The World the World Should Be

a utopian novel
by Willie Watson

also by Willie Watson:
This Book Contains Bad Language
Nice and Spicy
Recycling
Dark
Possibly the Shallowest, Most Pointless, Irrelevant,
and Trivial Book of Poetry Ever Written
Circle of Happiness
Diamonds on Uranus
Sentience
A Country' s Just a Place
Everyday's a Butterfly
Cup of Tea
The Quest for Enlightenment and Stuff
Paradox
Wild Pigs of Fukushima
The Meaning of Life in Easy English
Geology
Pink Snow
155 Sonnets
Uncle Willie´s Very Silly Animal Poems
The This of the That
Tarot Poems (with Marie Brožová)
The Alchemist´s Notebook
Four Syllables on Water
The Guru Kalehuru and Other Poems
Poems from Prague

Thanks to www.pixabay.com/geralt for the cover photo

In Utopia there is no war,
oppression or pollution
for every single problem
we've discovered the solution

There are vibrant, gleaming cities
there are pleasant little towns
the air is fairly ringing
with all the happy sounds

a cottage in the forest
a village by the sea
custom made for everyone
how happy we will be!

Utopia, Utopia
it won't be hard to get used to
and we could have this world tomorrow
if we'd only choose to

March 30th, The Future

Chapter 1

It's not a crime, it's not a sin
some people just do not fit in

Dan de Leon, 15, looked down on perfection, both literally and figuratively. He had a good vantage point, sitting on a cool, granite, slab bench near the summit of Buckminster Fuller Park, high on the green and flowering hill overlooking Wackturtle Bay, that is, both the bay and the town of the same name, on the southern shore of Lake Rub al Khali, a vast inland sea stretching out to infinity east and west, with just a dim line on the horizon to indicate the opposite shore, where a necklace of lights, from homes, hotels and the north shore road and railroad, appeared magically when the sky turned black.

Wackturtle Bay did not imply any cruelty to animals, or anything like that. At the town meeting to pick a name (because 243 South just wasn't cutting it) somebody had suggested Turtle Bay, because if you had a good imagination or a couple of drinks, it may have been said to resemble a turtle, in rough outline, and somebody else had said "Dude, that is one wack turtle." That name had stuck.

The bench was at the lower edge of a grove of figs, the oldest domesticated fruit tree in the world, a link to ancient times, and the massive green leaves made this, literally, a very cool spot. Behind that was the desalinization and pumping station, which was a small tourist site in its own right, as the salt water pumped from the lake was heated to steam and then ran down all four sides of the terraced tower in what some considered a large and impressive fountain and others saw it as a quaint, little waterfall. Its main purpose was the irrigation of the large, flat plain which stretched out to the mountains, about 50 kilometers distant, which were made of the stone that had been pulled out to create the lake and covered with topsoil created by all the new recycling centers. Nothing was wasted in Utopia.

The plain was a checkerboard of small farms bursting with vegetables and melons year-round.

The road and the railroad cut through it, but could barely be seen through the green, even though they weren't far away.

Dan was just an average looking guy, skinny and short for his age, which most people, upon meeting him, would guess at about two years younger than he was. He was smarter than most of the kids in his school, nobody disputed that, but fat lot of good it had ever done him.

From his vantage point, he looked down the hill, which descended like a giant's staircase, like the terraced rice paddies of Sri Lanka, short, steep slopes navigable by a few stairsteps, connecting a series of plateaus. The park was at least 3 times the size of the rest of the town. People were having picnics, and vendors were walking around selling battered shrimp, chicken, sausages, sushi, hot bread, steamed rice, wine by the glass or bottle, cold soft drinks and beer, pre-rolled joints, everything you might need. There were people playing frisbee, there was an old man playing mandolin by one of the fountains who had attracted a small crowd, a few other buskers and performance artists here and there, kids wading in the stream which wound its way down the park, and everybody was enjoying the nice sunny day, which most days here were.

Further down, there was a large children's playground or a small amusement park, depending on your perspective, a skate park, a mini-golf course, and a stadium, all with a bit of space between them as the park melded into the town and it wasn't that clear where one ended and the other began. Either side of the park were the garden homes, and that's where almost half the town's people lived.

They had trees and bushes, and their flat roofs were covered with herbs and flowers, many had small orchards and trellised gardens, almost all had a marijuana bush or two, for personal use, family and friends, some maybe selling a bit on the open market but since high-grade, mind-bending quality pot was growing all over the planet, there really wasn't a great deal of profit in it. Quite a few had chickens, or goats, each one was a little different but, seen in this quilt like pattern, all were very much the same. These continued up the sides of the park, getting a bit rockier, a bit larger, and having a few more goats and a bit less dense plant life as they moved up the hill.

Below them was the town itself.

It was not a big town. The whole town was less than two kilometers long. From where he sat he could easily pick out his school, the elementary school, the town hall, which was also the police station, which mostly existed just to give directions to tourists (there hadn't been any crime in years) and the hospital, which wasn't much more than a clinic, really, but was perfectly adequate for a community of hotels and local residents who almost never got sick, because of all the clean and comfortable housing, the pleasant, if a bit warmish climate, a healthy diet, plenty of outdoor activities, and plenty of check-ups through the school system, just like everywhere else. Then there was the market, including the fish restaurant his family owned and lived directly above. Dan worked there, it was a family thing, and he hated it like hell when kids from school would come in with their families. He was O.K. with the tourists. His parents, however, were extremely proud of it and, like everybody else in town would go on and on about 'this wonderful utopian world we live in.'

"Yeah, utopian if you like fish" Dan would say, and his father would tell him to stop being a smartass and his mother would say "You should be a bit more grateful, Danny."

Then there was the bay, with all of the sailboats, yachts, jet skis, and fishing craft, * some of which belonged to locals, but most of which were for renting to tourists. The town's population was less than 10,000 but the number of people in it could be almost double that, some days. Around the bay were a few guest houses, the Wackturtle Bay Hotel, a variety of restaurants, pubs, and cafes, parks, and beaches. Then a couple more residential blocks, and the parking garage (no cars were allowed in town except for deliveries, emergencies, and special cases which required a permit. Generally, pedestrians wandered the streets freely) and the bus depot, from where a bus left every 15 minutes, up the windy road to the ridgetop and through the fields, different colors in different seasons, to the train station and from there you could get to anywhere in the world in not too much time and for not too much money. Either side of town, for 5 or 6 kilometers hugging the shoreline, were the palatial estates and fancy yachts of the wealthy. The lots had sold for 2 million stacks** each, which had put them within reach of the only moderately wealthy, sometimes with a bit of financing. They had been snapped up, there were literally millions of them globally, and they'd paid for the whole lake construction project.

It was, overall, a prosperous town, and everybody who lived there felt prosperous. The streets were clean and neat, the food was exquisite, the weather was unfailingly warm, but the town had lots of shade, you could walk anywhere in less than 10 minutes, and there was almost always someplace open to buy whatever you needed.

It was a typical town in the post-transition world, it was perfect, and Dan was dark cloud bored of it.

"I can't wait to get out of this damned town," he thought.

He was to get his wish sooner than he expected.

---

*Just as with the land vehicles, all electric, of course. Nobody used gasoline as a power source anymore, and nobody missed it.

**Standard Currency Unit, which everybody called stacks because nobody's going to wander around saying 'standard currency units' when they're talking about how much they paid for something. Roughly similar in value to what a dollar or a euro was worth, in ancient times, before the transition.

Chapter 2

We should do away with the absolutely specious notion that everybody has to earn a living.

R. Buckminster Fuller

In the future, if you please
all the fields and factories
will have robot employees
who work for zero pay
and so, the people will be free
from drudgery, monotony
we'll all live lives of luxury
upon that glorious day
The sun will shine, the rivers flow
the rain will fall, the plants will grow
sometimes a gentle breeze will blow
and it will be O.K.

Veronika Vinohrady, 16, hated her parents. Well, maybe hate is too strong a word. Figure of speech. She knew her parents loved her, they absolutely doted on her, and her brothers. Resented might be a better word. Why in the world did they choose this pathetic life?

They lived in Peachy Valley, which was technically an artists' colony, but Veronika, and anybody else with eyes and any artistic sensibilities at all, could see that most of the neighborhood's residents, her parents not excluded, were loafers and posers. Her father played in a band, and they played around town, covers mostly. He'd never actually written a song. Her mother liked to paint, but it was a hobby she indulged in less and less often. Their house was full of stuff she could never sell. A lot of desert landscapes. Not terrible, just not original. Her parents barely even spoke Spanish, despite having lived here for most of their adult lives.

Peachy Valley itself was just one of the neighborhoods in Encatorce, so called because its official designation was N-14, or Nimbyille 14. Nimbyville's were a type of community set up at the beginning of the transition, filled with all the socially necessary institutions that everybody knew society needed but nobody wanted in their immediate vicinity, thus N.I.M.B.Y., or 'not in my backyard.' There were over a thousand of them worldwide, but they all had names, and their official designations, and their history, were often unknown even to their residents. Many, like Encatorce, had been especially constructed during the transition. Many others had been fading, dying communities which needed an infusion of employment to keep from becoming ghost towns.

Some, in fact most, had outgrown their negative foundations, much as Australia had outgrown its penal colony past. Encatorce was still kind of struggling with that.

The town consisted of a prison, a mental institution, the regional full scale recycling center and a nuclear power plant both of which were a bit north of town jutting out into the southern edge of the Sonoran desert which, up until the transition, had been right smack dab in the middle of the Sonoran desert, a shelter for abused women which was really more of a social club for women because the improved educational system and the elimination of poverty had reduced the amount of domestic abuse worldwide to the point where it was a rare anomaly, a retirement home, a golf course (which was adjacent to the retirement home), some low rent housing for the workers at the aforesaid facilities, and Peachy Valley. There were, as the name implied, a lot of peach trees, lots of other fruit trees, and a few community gardens, like the one around Peachy High. The people who lived there called it an artists' colony, and it was that, a bit, but since there was no requirement for being an artist except for saying you were one, it was not an overly impressive neighborhood, and Veronika was a bit embarrassed to live there.

She watched TV. She saw the homes and neighborhoods people lived in in the movies, saw people with real jobs, important jobs, elegant clothes, who ate in fancy restaurants, much nicer than the one in Peachy Valley, which was basically a soup kitchen. (There were better restaurants in Encatorce, in the neighborhoods where people worked and earned money, just not in Peachy Valley.) The food was not bad, the food was great and there was plenty of it, the vegetables were all bio and locally grown, but the atmosphere was kind of bland and there was no table service.

Veronika was turning out to be an extremely good looking girl, but nobody'd thought so until last summer. As a child, she'd been a total tomboy, and nobody thought of her as particularly attractive. For a while, as a budding adolescent, she'd been worried that she might not attract boyfriends because, at some point or another in their childhood, she'd beaten the crap out of most of them. For a very short while. As soon as her breasts became visible, they were all around her, and she could actually feel the heads turning as she walked down the hall at school. Older men, too. She was a magnet, and she kind of liked it.

Chapter 3

If you have built castles in the air, your work need not be lost; that is where they should be. Now put the foundations under them.

Henry David Thoreau

Smile, though you have no cash
to buy a lot of things
Smile, though your powerless
a puppet on a string
Smile when you're frustrated,
full of doubt, or just plain bored
Smile, because a smile is
it's very own reward

"You have to study, Olive" her mother had always told her growing up. "You can't get by on just a smile." So, Olive had. She'd done fairly well in school, especially in English and music, and at 14 had been accepted to an academy for the arts. She'd flirted with a career as a singer (she flirted with everybody, it came naturally to her and people seemed to like it), but when Olive Odhiambo got a gig as an announcer on Good Morning Nairobi, she took to the role like a frog to a big, mucky, algae ridden pond. She loved talking with the people, the entertainers, the athletes, the politicians, the people with strange hobbies, the people pushing odd causes, the fortune tellers, witch doctors, priests and people on the street.

She was, as our story begins, sitting at an outdoor café sipping a tall mint tea in the Moroccan section of World World, which was pretty much her favorite place in the world. A couple of hours from Nairobi by very scenic high speed rail, mostly along the southern coastline of Lake Sahara, and then the last half hour slowing down through the jungle canopy before emerging at Narirobi's New Central Station, an ultra modern but very green edifice within 20 minutes by self-driving taxi of either her studio, in the center of town, or her home, a rather palatial affair in an affluent suburb with lots of tropical gardens, where her husband, who was also one of her cameramen, was currently watching their three children – a girl, 8, and two boys, 5 and 3. Roger was a prince. She felt lucky, and blessed, and not guilty at all about being away from her family. It was only for three days, but oh, she intended to enjoy it. They were here to cover a Mongolian arts festival and, this evening, to moderate a panel discussion on the future of the Himalayas with representatives from all the countries in the region. Then, her boss had promised her two days of just wandering around with a camera crew, which was what she liked best. You never knew who you were going to find, but you almost always found somebody interesting.

Yes, she had it made. A great job, a wonderful family, a big house, plenty of money...and, she reflected with a certain degree of smugness, she had done it all on just her smile. She sometimes teased her mother about that, but not too much. She also knew she'd been lucky.

It must be said, she had a magnificent smile, a 100-watt smile, a contagious smile, a welcoming smile that put everyone within 100 meters at ease, and it was her stock in trade. It contrasted with her nearly black skin like a sun in the night. It hypnotized, and even the perviest men couldn't take their eyes off it, keeping their line of sight north of her bosom, which was, undeniably, ample. Oh, so very ample. She was pretty, few would disagree, but the overall impression was motherly, and she liked that that was a part of her public image. She'd kept on working through all of her pregnancies, keeping the public updated about all the details, and breastfed her children in the middle of her show, just as casual as could be. The public adored her for it, but her journalistic style was also of the likeable variety. She didn't ask hard questions. It wasn't that kind of show. She was a fluff journalist, and she was totally fine with that.

World World was, according to some people, just a huge theme park, a permanent World Fair, and to others a very gimmicky suburb to Timbuktu, which was the capitol city of Earth. Situated on the southern shore and near the western end of Lake Sahara, it was chosen because it was not within the territory of any large or powerful country which was a threat to anybody else or ever had been, it had a pleasant year round climate, (which would have been prohibitively hot before the lake was there, but now it was just right), it was not in an area prone to earthquakes, volcanoes, or tropical storms, it was flat enough to make construction of the airport and rail lines easy, and it was a paradise for bicyclists. It was a green city, with lots of parks among the monumentally large, stone, government buildings.

World World was adjacent, twenty kilometers long and right across the street, plenty of people lived in one and worked in the other. It had about 100,000 permanent residents, about 20,000 each in little India and Little China. Smaller nations had proportionally smaller sections. Luxembourg, for example, just had about 100 people, living in the area of one city block. There was one hotel, in a picturesque 3 story cabin. Old world outside, with 28 luxurious, spacious rooms, a restaurant, and a conference room on the inside. There were a couple of other residential buildings, and the rest was a public garden.

Each country could use the space as they saw fit, but most had cultural centers to show their best face to the world, a few restaurants, and a business center. World World was a great place to have a convention, or negotiations, and it had come to be kind of a people's U.N., certainly a place that the politicians in Timbuktu could go to get a whiff of public opinion, and people of all countries were close enough to Timbuktu to make their voices heard on any matter they cared about deeply. Perhaps the most important aspect of it was that, as each nation put its best foot forward, musically, architecturally, gustatorily, and in customer service, a beautiful whole grew out of the disparate parts and a Disneyfied fantasy vision of the world as people wanted it to be, a tangible vision for the future that existed in real time in the physical universe, a beacon showing the path forward, began to emerge.

Also, businesspeople and entrepreneurs loved the fact that they could make global contacts so easily there. A Korean manufacturer of androids could meet with a Bollywood director, a group of Nigerian farmers, some Russian space scientists, and the owner of an international chain of brothels all on the same day.

In fact, that was happening on the day our story begins. Robonerd and Madame Moiselle were seated not far away from our protagonist, but there was no eye contact between the two tables, she wasn't eavesdropping on their conversation (as she often, admittedly, liked to do) and it's not relevant to the story at all.

A limousine pulled up in front of the restaurant, followed by the camera crew, makeup artists, and everybody else in a van that had "Good Morning, Nairobi!" in huge letters on the side amid a garish collage of scenes and faces.

Olive flagged a waiter, paid her bill with a generous tip (expense account, she could add that to the list; She had a great job, a wonderful family, a big house, plenty of money, and an expense account) and got in. "What do I need to know?" she said, without bothering to say good morning or how do you do. Kirby was so often by her side, it was like he was never gone, and the conversation between them was continuous, so hellos and good byes would have been superfluous.

Kirby Brian was a balding man in his mid–30s, extremely fit because he spent most of his free time in the gym, although even there, he remained connected, his headset always plugged in and the gym he went to had screens all over the place. He was totally dedicated to Olive, which she knew and took advantage of shamelessly. He was the Alfred to her Batman, the Sam to her Frodo, the Smithers to her Burns.

"There will probably be a lot of that throat-singing stuff, you'll have to pretend to like that, but also a fashion show and a pretty good buffet, just have fun with it, you'll be great, we'll have lunch there and stay till about 2 o'clock and then we've got a few free hours before the panel discussion, I suggest we go back to the hotel and get in some research and practice your speech a bit..."

"I'm suggesting we go back to the hotel and I practice up on my sleep, if that's all right."

"Sure, if that's what you want." Kirby knew that she really didn't need too much prep, and he also knew that she wouldn't get more than 45 minutes of sleep before she was on her feet, firing off questions about the topic, practicing her lines, and fidgeting about her wardrobe. She was a natural, she always came up with just the right line on stage, just the right facial gesture to make her guests feel at home, to calm people who were at odds, to make the reticent loquacious, but she was also a professional, and didn't ignore the behind– the– scenes stuff.

"What about after the conference. Any big plans for the evening? Maybe dinner at Le Poulin Rouge and then over to Chez Guevara in Cubaville for drinks and dancing?"

From his hesitation, she knew that something was wrong.

"What?"

"Bad news on that front, I'm afraid. Well, maybe good news, too, but they want you back in the studio tomorrow. Ellen Celery is in town and you're the one they want interviewing her. We could still do dinner, but we should catch a night flight right after that."

"Ellen Celery! That's great news. She's huge! I'm a big fan of her music, it'll be great to meet her. I'm sure I'll get back to World World again soon. Should bring the kids some time. Let's skip dinner and take the train."

"As you wish."

"I sleep better on the train."

Chapter 4

*Not everyone is fair of face
or swift, or smart, or strong
but everyone should have a place
a place where they belong*

Todd Katz was not an attractive man and had the personality of a cactus. He'd had a crappy home life as a child, and it wasn't much better at school. He was an average student, an indifferent athlete, and not popular at all. Not hated so much, just generally ignored. By the age of 16, he was a homeless drug addict on the streets of Detroit, and well known to the police, who he figured would probably kill him some day.

He was the first to admit that the Everybody Gets a Job program, which was a project of the United Nations, had saved his life. It was aimed mostly at people in the 3rd world, in places like Africa and India, where there were way more people than jobs, but it really helped the desperately poor people in developed countries, too.

He'd first been sent to Siberia, planting trees along

the methane corridor, that line running through Russia, Canada, and Alaska where global warming posed a specific threat to mankind, both because the melting of the permafrost would release huge amounts of methane into the atmosphere, but also because this ground, which had been iced over with life held inert for several thousand years, could release bacteria against which human beings had no natural defense.   A bare 10 kilometers wide, the AMF (anti-methane forest, known also as the AML, from the Russian) stretched for well over 10,000 kilometers, and contained billions of trees, mostly pine, spruce, aspen, birch, and oak, the sacred tree of both the Celts and the Vikings, and so many sugar maples that maple syrup had overtaken both sugar and honey to become the world's most popular sweetener, although each had their particular adherents and their specific niche in the world of gourmet confectionary.

The fresh air and lack of access to hard drugs (plenty of marijuana available, and half the crews were stoned half the time, but the trees all still got planted) helped him get straight and the food wasn't bad, it beat the hell out of scrounging in garbage cans, but he hadn't made many friends (People wax poetic about how travel broadens their view of the world and how making friends from different cultures helped them discover that all people, at heart, are the same. What Todd had discovered was that people from all countries were just as much assholes as those he'd known at home). The work wasn't difficult, but he found it boring, so when winter came and almost everybody was sent elsewhere, he was happy to go. They sent him to Syria, which was still a mess from the late pre-transition period, when it had been grievously tortured by war, earthquakes, and the criminality and tribalism which followed. He'd worked on a cleanup crew, and rather liked it, but soon found himself working on the Hanging Gardens recreation project, which was part of the Restoration and Expansion of Monuments program (REMP), which was reinventing places like the hanging gardens, but modern and even more spectacular. There were many such projects around the world. Troy was now Troy the archeological site, and next to it a replica of Troy, but with modern toilets and showers and spacious rooms and gourmet restaurants, ditto with Tanis, Memphis, Akhetaten and Pi-Ramesses in Egypt, jewel bedecked palaces and reflecting pools galore, and Carthage, Timgad, and Leptis Magna on the very trendy southern coast of the Mediterranean. Then there were the monumental sites that no one wanted to change, but slums had been cleared and improvements made around them. The Taj Mahal now had a large number of luxurious hotels, and some homes, built in white marble and sporting domes and reflecting pools, for a 10 kilometer radius around it. A few ideologues had complained about gentrification, that the transitional government was just hiding poverty, keeping it away from the eyes of tourists, but the locals, who all got nice, new, luxury flats out of the deal, weren't complaining. Some, who still couldn't afford to live in the new neighborhood despite having a paid for home, just sold up and moved elsewhere. Everyone profited.

Sometimes Todd wondered if it wasn't a mistake to sanitize the world so much, if it wasn't causing people to becoming divorced from reality. Then he'd finish a hard day's work and sit relaxing in a hammam, preferably the kind with a big chonk of hashish permanently burning in the center, or just wander around the marketplace and treat himself to a kebab and chips, and he'd think of something else. He wondered about the future, and the fate of mankind, but he didn't care all that much.

On the lovely March day our story begins, he decided it was time to switch jobs again. His foreman was a bit of a pain in the ass, the project was nearly finished, he'd been there almost a year which was more than he'd ever spent on a job before, and he'd talked to a couple of guys who were working at a recycling plant and said it wasn't too bad. The pay was the same, and it was really easy to switch from one job to another within the Everybody Gets a Job Program. You could just fill in the paperwork online and show up the next day someplace else, ready to work. He figured he'd put in six months there, and then maybe try a different part of the world. But, it was to change his life.

Chapter 5

The greatest challenge to any thinker is stating the problem in a way that will allow a solution.
Bertrand Russell

If you want to get where you want to go
then you need to follow the map
If we don't have a plan for the future
then, the future will be crap

This is how the transition began: Artificial intelligence, after a great deal of trial and error, had become sophisticated enough that when somebody typed in: "Based on a human population of ten billion, please design a system which will provide every human being on Earth with unlimited fresh water, breathable air, an adequate and healthy food supply, comfortable housing, comfortable and reliable global transportation, state of the art health care, and the opportunity to get as educated as he or she is capable of, and to do so sustainably for as long as the planet known as Earth shall exist. This system should include a worldwide government which is democratic, representative, and limited so as to preserve each individual's rights and autonomy, and a physical infrastructure which is both in tune with the natural environment and aesthetically pleasing. Include provisions for the preservation of all human cultures, and the preservation of the natural environment. Please also include a plan for transitioning from our current world society to the new one, which does not include force or coercion of any kind.

The figure of ten billion had been chosen for three reasons. First, because at that time it was estimated that the human race would reach that ugly milestone in a few years, secondly because it seemed as if we went much higher than that, it wouldn't matter what we did, the Earth's resources wouldn't be able to cope. It was Malthusian logic, but Malthus was not wrong. Whether the figure is 10 billion, 20 billion or 30 billion, there is definitely a number beyond which we cannot go. The third reason was that it was a nice, round number and easy to calculate from. This did not make a bit of difference to the AI, but it did make sure the response was easier for people to understand.

Approximately 12 hours later, the task was completed. A 4,682 page document, entitled simply "Plan for an Improved Human Civilization," including a constitution, a list of materials and labor costs, blueprints for brand new environmental cities and towns in a wide variety of configurations based on climate, function, and lifestyle choices, and plans for redesigning the current large urban centers with large green areas, public squares, fountains, and adequate public transportation, was put forth upon the internet for all to read or download.

It left large areas of the Earth alone, mostly as nature reserves but also as refuges for those who didn't want such an ordered society. (The AI estimated that 1.8% of the world's population would prefer to live in a shack in the woods with no electricity and running water than in a perfectly managed society. In the end, it was off by less than 1%)

It even included an outline of the various projects and programs which would be necessary to achieve that goal.

It was pretty much ignored. Eventually, however,

it became impossible to ignore the threat of a changing global climate. After the great flood of Manhattan, and Hurricane Zaphod, which had circumcised America's penis right up to Fort Lauderdale, and the summer that everybody just referred to as 'the long, hot summer' which killed tens of millions, it became impossible to ignore the problem.

An international environmental task force was formed, and they soon found that everything that needed to be done was already in the plan. It still took a long time to implement, human nature being stubborn to the point of self-destructive, delusional to the point of suicidal. There were objections on the grounds of national sovereignty, religion, aesthetics and all sorts of other stuff, but the plan not only was a blueprint for saving the environment but would directly and materially benefit every individual on the planet, even the stinking rich bastards who were ready to see the human race fry before giving up any of their power. So, some aspects of the plan started to be implemented, and then others, and then others. Full transition to a utopian world took a couple of decades, but it happened. And everybody lived as happily ever after as they could.

Chapter 6

Let's focus on what we can do
forget about the rest
and in the end, I'm sure that things
will work out for the best

In this book I present solutions to hunger, homelessness, war, injustice, oppression, traffic jams, road rage, parking, desertification, soil degradation, littering, illiteracy, lack of health care, refugees, floods, drought, wildfires, hurricanes, and the threat of a rogue asteroid striking the Earth.

What follows are some of the issues I have chosen not to address, and my reasons for not doing so.

Undoubtedly, one of the main obstacles to creating such a perfect world, such a utopia of abundance, is overpopulation, but I'm not going to deal directly with it in this book, for a couple of reasons.

One is that it would be very wrong, both tactically and morally, for any government, or even society as a whole, to try and tell people when or how many children they can bring into this world. That is, and should always be, a personal choice.

Another is that I think it is a problem which will solve itself in time.

It's sort of obvious that one way to solve a problem is to look and see if it has already been solved somewhere, and then emulate whatever they are doing. There are several countries in the world where the birth rate is dropping, where the population is decreasing year by year. (Astoundingly, there are some people in those countries who see that as a problem, but it is not. The idea should be to bring the rest of the world up to their level.) Discounting those countries where the population is dropping because of war, famine, or people just want to get the hell out of there, the rest are countries where the population is decreasing because the standard of living is high and people have great opportunities to go to university and build a career, (and party in clubs and have lots of passionate love affairs with random strangers) and not settle down and have kids until their 30s. This is already a utopian situation.

I also don't deal with the issue of racism. It is mathematically indicated that it's going to just plain die out within a few more generations. It's like this: There are, even today, millions, maybe hundreds of millions of people out there who are of mixed race. People who are half Asian and half white, half white and half black, half black and half Asian, or hundreds of other exotic combinations. Sometimes it's hard for them, they're still a minority, but no longer a rarity. They are in Hollywood, they are in the music scene, they are moving forward in every aspect of life. They are doctors, they are lawyers, they are merchants, they are cops. They, in turn, will have children who are mixed race, while a few newcomers join their ranks. Their numbers can only increase, never decrease, because children of mixed children will still be mixed, maybe even more mixed, but never unmixed. Their numbers are going to increase even faster as the speed of transportation and communication increases, and personal mobility becomes greater. The system proposed in this book is really, really big on personal mobility – personal physical mobility due to the international public transportation grid, personal social mobility due to the removal of national boundaries, and personal economic mobility due to the educational system. In a few generations, nobody will be able to slag off another race even in private conversations, because everybody will be so mixed that you'll never know. Race will become, eventually, completely irrelevant.

I'm also not going to talk about religion. That's partly because, like racism, organized religion is decreasing in influence at a steady rate and will continue to do so.

More importantly, though, the system I'm about to propose doesn't violate any basic religious precepts, except maybe Santeria and Satanism, because of animal sacrifice. The system would work equally well in a devoutly religious world as it would in a totally atheistic world.

There are a few other issues I have chosen to ignore, such as abortion, guns, daylight savings time, and who gets to use which bathroom, because, as with religion, the system I am proposing will work whichever way we come down on these issues.

It's not that I don't have my personal opinions. I am pro-choice, anti-gun, think daylight savings time is kind of stupid but don't really care, and that everybody should use whichever restroom is most appropriate to the current state of their genitalia and everybody else should just mind their own business. But that's the last I'm going to say about any of those. They aren't important to this book; they aren't important to a future utopian society.

Chapter 7

When things change for the better
then we know that we're on track
and there's no way in hell
that we are ever turning back

Dan was looking, and trying not to look like he was looking. There was quite a large crowd in front of the auditorium doors, slowly filing in. His friends (Friends! He had friends, a gang, a crew, a posse.) He hadn't admitted that to himself even yet. It had all happened so fast and was just based on them living in the same house, but it filled him with a newfound sense of wellbeing and confidence. It was a feeling he liked. They had agreed to meet here, and they should have been here by now, so either he was late, or they were.

He'd only been at Rocklaw Academy two days, and he already felt at home. It was a lovely campus, very old school, large brick buildings, shaded walkways and wide green lawns. It was in an old city, over a thousand years old, in the middle of Europe. There were lots of cities like this in Utopia.

Statuesque 19th century buildings, bottom lit at night and reflected in the slow-moving river, very soft and romantic. By day the preponderance of stone and brick gave them a feeling of permanence, and reassurance. These were real cities, but they had been affected by the transition less than most. Traffic was light, because of public transportation, and most of the important stuff being within walking distance, and bicycles being popular. There was no problem with garbage, because of the universal recycling program, adequate but attractively designed trash receptacles, and the little trash eating robots which looked like pot belly pigs with an elephant's trunk and roamed the city's sidewalks during off-peak hours. The city was squeaky clean, like every other place on Earth. There was no problem with homelessness, because those people had moved on, either into the Everybody Gets a Job program or appropriate psychological institutions, surrounded by gardens and trees which were pumping oxygen into the air, and not bothering anybody at all. Other than those tiny, almost unnoticed subtractions, the city looked much as it had for the past few hundred years.

Dan had met a lot of people, but still only knew his roommates, and really didn't want to sit on his own. This was a new environment. This was a new thing, and the last thing he wanted was to fall into his old, anti-social pattern. A week ago, sitting on his own wouldn't have fazed him, he was used to it. Now, he dreaded it.

His phone dinged. '3 rows from the front, leftish' With a sigh of relief that he hoped wasn't audible, he walked through the nearest doors, scanned the room, and saw them right away.

By the time he reached his seat, nearly everybody was inside. The auditorium wasn't full, it could hold the entire school and more. This was just the welcoming assembly for the first-year students. A handful had staked out individual seats, like islands in a nearly empty ocean, but the vast majority were clumped near the front, and centered.

The first couple of days had left him very impressed by the campus, very green, very classy, very comfortable, and reasonably impressed by the student body, those he'd met had been friendly enough, and there were plenty of good looking girls. Of the teachers they'd met, none had seemed tyrannical, and both students and teachers had been forthright about answering most of their questions - except one. Nobody had been able to figure out why they were selected for this school, what kind of school it actually was, and nobody was telling them. It was kind of weird. A lot of them thought it was high IQ, but those they'd asked had flatly denied that, and he didn't think they were lying.

The program basically consisted of a speech by the Dean, with lots of very prosaic language about the best years of their lives, and the school preparing them for great and brilliant futures, and he had begun to doubt there would be any specific clues in the speech as to the why of it all and he had begun to drift into that mental state where the speaker was just background noise and time was temporarily suspended. A few people were actually nodding off.

So, he was a bit startled when the speech, which he had begun to think would never end, ended, and the Dean asked if there were any questions. He looked around to see which student would be bold enough to ask and was quite surprised, and more than a little disappointed, to see no one. So, quite tentatively, he raised his hand, still somehow hoping that someone else would be called upon. "Yes, the young man in the 3rd row with the blue shirt and latent leadership qualities." All eyes turned to him, and Dan had a strong desire to stand up and run from the room, but that would have been a long and pointless gauntlet to run. "Wh-why are we here?"

"You're going to have to be a bit more specific. If you're asking why human beings exist in the universe, that will be covered in your philosophy classes. If you're asking why we are here in this assembly, it's because it's mandatory."

"How is it that we were selected for this school. What was the criteria? What kind of school is this?"

"Ah, yes. There we go. That's the question. First of all, don't give yourselves too much credit. Some of you are very smart, none of you are stupid, that's true. But it's not an elite academy, it's not a genius school. There are lots of those, but this isn't one. Also, you are not unique. There are dozens of schools like this one around the world. So, you're not special, except in the way that all human individuals are special. In fact, you were all chosen because of a flaw you all share, and none of your positive attributes."

He paused here, took a deep breath, grabbed the podium at either side, leaned forward, and spoke, clearly and distinctly, so there could be no mistake. "You are all losers. None of you had a social life, or any real friends. Oh, some of you might have had a couple people you thought of as friends, but they won't miss you, they'll barely even notice you're gone. You were, in some cases, mistaking tolerance for genuine acceptance."

Nobody was snoozing any more, that was for sure.

Chapter 8

Education is the passport to the future, for tomorrow belongs to those who prepare for it today.

Malcolm X

Intelligence implies an urgent yearning
for ever more, and ever greater learning

Of course, fixing and stabilizing the Earth's environment had been priority number 1, back at the start of the transition, and giving everybody a home was also very immediate and urgent, and it was the establishment of a global, self-sustaining energy grid which paved the way for the global water system, the global transportation system, and the global recycling system, in short, all of those things which kept the Utopian economy chugging along, but it was the educational system which was the jewel in the crown, the thing which meant that Utopia was not a dead end, but would be succeeded by greater and greater Utopias as each generation built on the one before and humanity looked ever further out into the vast universe, and ever deeper into the atomic structure that makes up all the plants, animals and material of the universe.

While all those other things made it possible for people to live and thrive, it was the educational system which allowed them to grow. Despite its large percentage of the overall budget, people had become used to it, people loved it, and the evidence of its worth was demonstrated in small and large ways every single day.

To start with, it was universal, and comprehensive. Everywhere around the Earth, from the smallest village to the most remote island, people had the opportunity to go to school. Parents could enroll their children in the system from birth, although child care up to about year 4 was basically baby-sitting. The teachers would sing to them and read to them, and make sure they weren't too bad to the other babies, but they didn't have to have a degree in education or psychology. Sometimes they were students in those disciplines, sometimes they were older people who just loved babies. A background check was required, but that was about it.

From age 4 up until university, class size was limited to a dozen. For one thing, this gave each teacher a lot more time to devote to each individual student, it made classroom discipline much easier, and made sure everyone was part of a tight, cohesive social unit from a very young age. There was one other reason for this. The teachers, armed with a few psychology courses and a checklist of symptoms, could easily spot the future psychopaths, the anti-social loners, and take appropriate action. This meant they were doing double duty as social workers. There were the occasional parents who were insulted, aggrieved, and outraged, but they were almost always in the wrong. Parents are blinded by love and that is usually a good thing, a positive thing, but there are cases when society needs to take a more objective view.

About 12 years after the program had been fully implemented (which did take a few years – some of those remote villages were very remote indeed, and some parents still wanted to home school, which was still allowed (the constitution did specify that none of Utopia's goals were to be achieved by force or coercion) but regulated, and others preferred private schools and religious institutions, but they were a small minority as there is a huge difference between free and prohibitively expensive, and the quality of education in public schools with small classes and the most modern techniques was really hard to beat. Crime rates plummeted, especially the weird, violent, psychopathic type crimes. Not the main goal of an educational system, perhaps, but a happy byproduct of one that worked well. Children got educated in the basics, of course, reading, writing, arithmetic, geography, history, a bit of basic science, but also music, art, sports, drama, camping, caring for animals, basic DIY skills, gardening, and cooking. Speaking of gardening and cooking, every school had its own garden, where the children and teachers worked together, and the kids took part in preparing their own meals as well. Also, and by the way, every school, from elementary level up to universities, had on campus housing for teachers, which was a nice little perk because no matter how much teachers were paid, it could never be enough, but throw in a somewhat better than average flat and it was, most teachers agreed, a pretty sweet deal. It also meant they didn't have to commute, and there was a similar deal for hospital employees. It reduced traffic, and crowding on public transport, and made everybody's life much easier.

At a fairly early age, students were allowed to specialize according to their needs and desires. There were schools, like the one Dan de Leon was attending, where there was an added emphasis on socialization, there were genius academies, schools for the performing arts, writers' schools, technical schools to learn plumbing, or electrical work, or computers, or construction and architecture, or engineering. The goal of education is not to make everybody the same, to make them rigidly conform to the societal norm, but to make everybody the best them that they can be, so the vistas of the human race can expand in every direction there is, even some we haven't thought of yet.

At the university level, it was still free, and since nobody needed to work to survive, lots of people were opting to delay their entry into the work force until they could do so with qualifications, and get a really good income.

At the post graduate levels, this meant that research into every scientific discipline known to mankind (and new ones were being opened up on the regular) thrived. This led to a state of steady innovation, which kept driving the economy forward. Some economists claimed it was a bubble, but it was one that showed no sign of bursting and if it did, nobody would starve or become homeless, because all that was just plain over.

Some people remained in the educational system their whole lives. Some wrote books, some taught classes, some engaged in scientific research, and some were pretty useless, but everybody was happy, which was sort of axiomatic, because if somebody wasn't happy, they could always do something else until they were.

Chapter 9

We never know what's in the minds
of those who are around us
if it were suddenly revealed
I think it would astound us

Can anybody tell me what they are?"

"Is there anybody who can't tell you what they are?" Veronika thought and mumbled under her breath. Professor Forbes was her least favorite professor. and the Utopian Constitution was one of her least favorite courses, although that was mostly because of Professor Forbes. He mostly just read from the book, or from the constitution itself, as he was doing now, and Veronika suspected it was just out of plain laziness. She'd been quite surprised when she was talking to her friends yesterday afternoon and found out that not everybody agreed.

"Easy A," Eduardo had said. He lets you know what's going to be on the tests, he's totally predictable. I just sit in the back and play Chatbat and he doesn't even care."

"At least he doesn't think he's some kind of life

style guru," Beth said, "like so many of them do."

"He's a negative life-style guru if anything. I hope I never get to be as boring as that," Veronika said, but she wasn't about to press the point. If they liked him, they liked him.

Several students had their hands in the air.

Forbes didn't call on any of them. He went straight to Armando Mendoza. Armando was the biggest kid in the class, and possibly the dumbest. Veronika had known him since kindergarten. He'd been a bit of a thug even then, but when he kicked over the palace she'd so lovingly built in the sandbox, she'd punched him in the forehead and knocked him on his butt. The other kids laughed, and the teacher broke it up quickly, but he never bothered her again, and in fact they'd become quite good friends over the years.

Lately, he'd been looking at her like all the other boys looked at her, and she was wondering if she should let him be the first. He wasn't bad looking, and she trusted him more than a lot of the others.

"What, Mr. Mendoza, are the six basic goals of our utopian society, as laid out in the constitution?"

He didn't answer right away. 'Come on, Armando'

she pleaded silently. 'Don't be a jerk, you'll be lucky to get a C in this class.'

He shrugged his shoulders.

"Can you give us one?," Forbes said, with a bit more than a hint of cruel sarcasm.

Nothing.

Veronika was a bit shocked. Could it be he didn't know? They'd studied this every year since the fifth grade. She had it memorized. She assumed everybody had.

He then went on to Charlie Baumgartner. Same blank look. Lucy Givens. She apologized for not knowing, but it wasn't a very sincere apology.

"Sorry, professor. Why don't you ask one of those with their hands up?"

Veronika was in disbelief. How was it possible that none of them knew? Were they really, truly that incapable of learning? It was an eye-opening moment and Armando was definitely out of the running in the potential first serious boyfriend competition.

Eventually, he called on Barbie Chan who, like Veronika, knew all the answers but, unlike Veronika, enjoyed showing off. They were good friends.

"The first goal is the maintenance of a life sustaining environment on Earth because everything depends on that. Next is the preservation of life on Earth, in its many and diverse forms. Third is the survival of the human race. Fourth is the survival of human individuals. Fifth is the comfort and convenience of human individuals. Sixth is the pursuit of knowledge, and constant improvement of the human race." She recited.

Veronika barely heard her. This had been an extremely educational moment for her, and her determination to leave Encatorce for the big wide world as soon as she turned 18 was re-enforced, like times a thousand.

Chapter 10

Capitalism's grow or die imperative stands radically at odds with ecology's imperative of interdependence and limits. These two imperatives can no longer co-exist with each other... Either we establish an ecological society, or society will go under for everyone.

Ursula LeGuin

The world is like a jigsaw puzzle
things fit in with other things
and when they click and snap together
Oh! What happiness it brings

When the Everybody Gets a Job program was instituted, it was a godsend for Todd, a lifeline, the luckiest break in the world. He got to try a lot of jobs, see a bit of the world and, most importantly, he wasn't sleeping outdoors and eating out of garbage cans. His health had improved, his addiction problems had been mastered, and he'd even started saving a bit.

The recycling business, however, was something

different for him and he was something different for it.   Many people considered it gross and demeaning, some couldn't handle the workload because the garbage came into the plant in a never ending deluge, this was the sphincter of humanity's digestive system, the waste of the every day lives of millions of people, and it needed to be sorted, sifted through, resorted, separated, processed, across an elaborate system of belts, wheels, sieves, pools, spinners and magnets, until it was finally processed and stored as compost, which would help in desert reclamation, landscaping, and restoring the environment of planet Earth to its prehistoric glory, glass, much of which was smashed and rolled around in centrifuges until it became smooth and shiny jewelry, but a lot just got recycled as glass, rubber which went into sandals and playground equipment, plastic, metal, cloth, reparable household items et cetera and there were a whole lot of ceteras.

Some items would be patched up and passed on to Thrift Stores, very cheaply but it was a bit of profit for the center, plastic and metal and paper would go through a bit of basic recycling but then sold on in bulk to factories which needed it, and again, that was a small part of the revenue stream, but still it was dependent on government funding, which was fair. They kept the world clean.

The first month or so, Todd had worked in a lot of different departments, on the line sorting, pushing wheelbarrows back and forth, stacking, carrying, sweeping, showing up on time and not taking excessive breaks. He was a model employee. Not that he was trying to be, he certainly didn't want to make anybody else look bad, and felt no particular loyalty to his bosses, but he actually enjoyed the work. Gradually, he became known in each department as the guy who could get anything from the other departments, which wasn't actually a job description, he was still low man on the totem pole, but he was making connections and all around him, and the turnover was rapid. Few people did this job for more than a month or two, and more than a few quit as soon as they got their first paycheck.

He was in his third month on the job when he discovered an unused room, in a corner at the back of the plant, which had a door that opened onto the loading dock, and he saw a way to improve the operation tremendously, and maybe make a side profit.

He checked in on his friends in plastics, and asked if they could let him have a few spare pop bottles. "Sure," the first person he talked to said. "Take as many as you like." He'd have got the same answer from anybody.

He took about a dozen wheelbarrows full, and it wasn't enough to notice.

Then he went to metals, and asked if he could take any old cans, didn't even need to be washed yet. "Sure," the first person he talked to said. "Take as many as you like." He'd have got the same answer from anybody. He took about a dozen wheelbarrows full, and it wasn't enough to notice. The he went to the WPC (waxy paper cartons) department and asked if he could take a few milk and juice cartons. "Sure," the first person he talked to said. "Take 'em all." He'd have got the same answer from anybody, because they were a bitch to recycle. They were cut open and then all the waxy bit inside had to be scraped off. There was a machine for that, but it was time consuming to feed them into the machine one by one. The waxy bits went to making candles, but that wasn't profitable. There was neither a shortage of candles in the world or an aching desire for more of them. So, he took all of them and that gave them a breather for a day or two.

Then, he walked out the back door with a wheelbarrow to the mountain of compost and asked if he could take some of their reconstituted soil and the foreman said "No, we've got customers for all that, and back orders," so he said "Can I take a bunch of raw compost and a little bit of soil?"

"You can take all the raw compost you want, we've got more than we can handle, you know that. There's a pile of dirt over there, you can have a bit of that, but none of the finished product."

"O.K., that's cool."

When he had all this he started filling the containers and planting seeds, all sorts of seeds, vegetables, bamboo, trees, flowers, bushes. He realized he'd need some lights and an irrigation system, and maybe some help, but he'd figure it out.

Then he got called into the boss's office.

He'd never met the boss, but he had heard that he was a stickler for the rules. He walked to the office with a sense of dread. He wasn't too worried about losing the job, he could start over in another place, but he hated the idea of losing the experiment.

"Go right in, Mr. Katz. Mr. Corey is waiting for you." Was that sarcasm he heard in her voice? Condescension?" Whatever it was, it didn't improve his mood.

The boss was a bland looking middle-aged man who looked, quite definitely, as if he'd never actually spent a second of his life sorting garbage. Todd hated him immediately.

"Sit," he said, and Todd did, although the tone of voice was like he was telling a dog to sit. "Explain yourself."

So, Todd did. The idea was to take small containers, which were a pain to recycle and unprofitable, fill them with compost, of which they had a surplus which was a constant problem, and a bit of raw dirt for appearances, and raise a lot of plants, which could be sold for almost nothing and still make more of a profit than the dirt and containers.

"Show me," Mr. Corey said.

When he saw the operation, he didn't say anything for a while. 'Jesus, just fire me if you're going to,' Todd thought. He couldn't take much more of this suspense.

"Well, on the one hand, I can't have you just deciding this stuff on your own. It was way outside of your job assignment. But, on the other hand, it's brilliant. You'll need lights, and a better irrigation system than just you walking around with a watering can, and you'll need a crew. I'm taking you off the line and making you head of the garden department. You'll report to me, regularly, and get approval for any changes. You're admin now, so you'll get a bit more money, too. O.K?"

"Yes, sure, of course. Uh, thank you, sir."

He'd created a new department.

Chapter 11

Sometimes a shock, a big surprise
happens, to make you open your eyes

When Olive's train pulled into Nairobi station, she still had 4 hours before she needed to report to the studio, so she caught a driverless to her home. She didn't ring the bell. Why make the maid come to the door when she had keys? She was rich, but she'd never understood, much less adapted, the mentality of getting other people to do things for you just because you could.

She was not surprised at the silence. This time of day, the older kids were still at school, and little Charlie was either at pre-school, or somewhere with his grandmother. Roger might be at the studio, or he might still be asleep. She was a bit surprised that she didn't see the maid, but it was a big house and she might be anywhere. She took off her shoes at the door, not for stealth but just because she always did, nobody needed to keep their shoes on indoors.

Nonetheless, it meant she ascended the steps in

silence, and when she heard the noises from their bedroom, nobody heard her.

Later, she could not remember what she had been thinking as she approached the room, but as soon as she opened the door she had her phone up and was filming.

There were four people in the room, and three of them were women. Well, one was little more than a girl, but she was certainly no innocent. The maid, Martha, was standing at the foot of the bed, bent over. Roger was standing behind her, naked except for a cowboy hat and doing her doggy style. Another girl, who Olive couldn't see very well but thought might be Asian, was lying underneath Martha, head to toe as the saying goes, but really more head to crotch, with Martha's face buried in hers and her tongue in the vicinity of Martha's hoo-haw and Roger's balls. 'That can't possibly be comfortable' Olive thought, surprising herself with how calm she was being. The third girl, a stunningly gorgeous blonde Barbie doll who didn't look a day over 18, was standing behind Roger with a riding crop, wearing part of Martha's uniform (the hat) lace panties and nothing else, occasionally giving him a swat on the butt and saying "Ride 'em, Cowboy! Yah! Yah!" It was probably only 3 or 4 seconds before the blonde wannabe starlet saw her there and let out a shriek which was obviously way off script.

The scene devolved quickly from there, it was amazing the alacrity with which everybody uncoupled and the two women she didn't know gathered their clothes and fled the room, never to be seen again, at least not by Olive.

Martha stood in front of her, clutching a blanket, shaking, with a stricken look on her face. "Please, ma'am...."

Olive knew exactly what she meant. Roger probably wouldn't be terribly bothered if the video went public, the jerk. And it would go viral. Sex, comedy, and she was just enough of a celebrity. But Martha was from the same neighborhood she was from and not likely to ever leave it. This would humiliate her in front of her family and friends and maybe scar her for life.

"All right," she said, holding up the phone to remind them of her leverage. "Here's what's going to happen."

Chapter 12

"Give me a place to stand, and a lever long enough, and I will move the world."

Archimedes

"You never change things by fighting the existing reality.
To change something, build a new model that makes the existing model obsolete."

R. Buckminster Fuller

Before the transition, whenever somebody would suggest desalination, or a worldwide rail network, or collecting and recycling all the world's plastic, the standard reply was "It would cost too much money."
A slightly closer examination would reveal that the primary cost, the thing that was making it cost too much money, was energy, but it was rare for anybody to make that slightly closer examination. So, little was done while the emissions from factories and the exhaust of literally billions of cars, continued to poison the air, threatening all

life on Earth.

So, that became the key point, the primary objective, the linchpin, the thing which made everything work in the great global transition plan. The first step in creating a clean global energy grid was to build what was easy. Parking lots in large, sunny cities such as Phoenix and L.A. were covered with solar panels, flat rooftops from Cairo to Christchurch, and wind turbines were set up the length and breadth of tornado alley and began to sprout up in cow pastures everywhere in the world that occasionally got more than a minor breeze. Tornadoes were no longer just natural disasters; they became a source of energy as well. Many urban areas with high foot traffic, and many roadways, were built to capture kinetic energy. Fitness centers had their treadmills and stationary bikes hooked up to the grid, but at the very most it kept their own lights on.

It wasn't enough. It was never enough. The AI had not made an error, really, it had calculated the world's energy needs as they were, but it seemed that every time energy production was increased to meet the demand, the demand, as if by magic, guided by an invisible hand, had also increased. The "Plan for a Better World" had underestimated the natural inflation rate of human greed, and the innate human (some humans) desire for bright lights and loud noises.

Then they'd put millions of solar panels out in space, beaming energy to all of the space stations, many of which were there just to accommodate wealthy tourists who still very much wanted to do things the average person couldn't do, and there was still energy left over to beam down to Earth, but not enough. Many offshore oil rigs were converted into floating solar farms, some of which also cultivated fish, and some of which operated as resorts for people who really, really wanted to get away from it all, but it still wasn't enough. Demand continued to increase.

Eventually, they'd been forced to amend the Plan for a Better World, and turn to nuclear. By that time nuclear had become much safer. Still, it made people nervous, so it was highly regulated. Nuclear plants were only built far away from fault lines, coastlines, and residential areas. They had large, thick earthen walls built around them, above ground sanitized landfills which were terraced for gardening at the outer side and had pleasant, tree lined walkways on top. They were also surrounded by wooded parks, not so huge that it made it difficult for anybody to get to work, but big enough to provide some nice picnic areas that could be evacuated quickly if there ever was a nuclear meltdown. The woods were also deep enough to absorb the radiation from such a disaster, so that there'd just be nothing left by the time it got to an area where people lived.but such a disaster hadn't happened in the last 20 years.

Bottom line, though, there was now plenty of energy, cheap enough that it was a negligible expense for the average homeowner, and entirely affordable for farmers and factory owners, and very profitable for the government, which was taking in enough from this, and the water rates, (which were also next to nothing for your average homeowner) and the luxury class tickets on the trains, and the government's stake in the recycling centers, and the fact that the government printed the money and calculated its value, there was no longer any need for taxes, and government employees had got raises in three of the last five years.

Chapter 13

The sea is vast and majestic
as lovely as it is grand
conveniently located
adjacent to the land

The sea is fun to play in
the sea is wild and free
when I am far away from it
it's where I long to be

It's been around forever
it's part of our sacred lore
the place of birth of life on Earth
a life that we adore

So, let's go for a walk along the beach
together, you and me
the sea, the sea is paradise
utopia is the sea

If you have the power of geo-engineering to turn Mars into Earth, then you have the power of geo-engineering to turn Earth back into Earth.

Neil deGrasse Tyson

The global water grid, a series of desalination and purification plants, pipes, pumps, canals, working in concert with the rivers, lakes, oceans, and the rain itself, was the greatest engineering and construction project the world had ever seen. It provided jobs for tens of millions of people, and once it was complete, hundreds of millions, because if you've got water, a bit of land, and the ever-loving sun above, you've got a farm, by golly, and farming was the root (pun intended) of the human economy and had been for about the last 70,000 years or so, nobody knows exactly. It became easy, once the grid was complete, to reclaim desert land, and turn it into farms and shady, luxurious resorts. Of course, all of the Earth's ecosystems exist for a reason in the interlinked web of life, so there were still portions of the Sahara, the Gobi, the Mojave, the Great Victoria, and many others that were preserved, along with all their species.

None were obliterated, but the world needed trees, food, and comfortable homes more, so new regions of green sprouted up.

Also, the current system of pipes and pumps was built, which could deliver water from anywhere to anywhere, so that water from flood areas is sucked right up before it can do much damage, and it's always there to stop a drought in its tracks or extinguish a forest fire. All the neighborhoods and schools in the future have bright, delightful swimming pools, there are drinking fountains everywhere you go (nobody needs to buy bottled water anymore), decorative fountains, mist machines, and sometimes waterfalls pouring down the sides of tall buildings, looking good and oxygenating the air. Hydroponic greenhouses have become common, and aquaculture is so common that during the late stages of the transition it was possible to declare a complete moratorium on ocean fishing, and now the oceans are absolutely teeming with fish again.

The most ambitious and impressive part of the program were the canals that became the thoroughfares of most low-lying coastal cities, which were lovely and created a great atmosphere but were also there for flood control as the water level was usually a little below peak, and the banks were often green spaces, perfect for picnics in nice weather and no harm, no foul if they got flooded occasionally, and the new inland seas, millions of kilometers of coastline, hundreds of millions of farms, which had both turned the desert green and created huge populations of some varieties of fish. These included Lake Tulare in California, the revived Aral Sea, and the two really huge ones, Lake Rub al Khali and Lake Sahara. Lake Rub al Khali is nearly in a straight line across what was once known at the empty quarter, with frequent bays containing moorage for luxury yachts and lovely, shallow swimming areas. From the air, it looks rather like a fat centipede. Lake Sahara has a somewhat more irregular coastline, and numerous islands which were formerly mountains. It starts in the northwest of Africa, just east of the Atlas mountains, and is fed by the Saguia el-Hamra canal, which begins at the port of El Ayoun in West Africa and ends where the lake begins, in Mauritania. It is a bulbous figure at that point, covering much of Mauritania and Mali, and reaching even reaching into Algeria a little bit. It continues across Niger and Chad, leaving several mountain peaks as islands, which became highly valued properties, because people like living on islands and several billionaires established their own little 'kingdoms' there, and up into the Libyan desert. Its easternmost point is on the border between Egypt and Sudan. The stone dug out was enough to build housing for all the farms and cities along the way, including the new world capital. The goal had been to decrease the ocean level a bit, but it had also set the stage for the creation of thousands of small, utopian communities and entire agricultural regions, flooding the world with mangoes, papayas, bananas, dates, figs, grapes, pomegranates, persimmons, oranges, tangerines and grapefruit, melons, watermelons, tomatoes, cucumbers, aubergines, zucchinis, and fish, oh, the fish, sport fishing was popular on the lake but there were also fish ponds all over the place producing all kinds of fresh and salt water fish, scaly fish, shell fish and cephalopods, not so much the big ones like sharks or marlin, but enough that fish had become the cheap meat everywhere in the world and the ocean's had had a chance to recover. The creation of lakes like this had also completely solved the refugee problem. Some areas were carved out as homelands for long oppressed groups, Zikanistan, South Kurdistan, Uighuria, and Tamilandia, among many others.

Particularly around the south shore of Lake Sahara, many warring tribes now had their own pockets of prosperity, separated from each other much in the way that you seat your religious fanatic relatives far away from the potheads at a wedding. New Palestine and New Zion were on opposite sides of the lake and hundreds of kilometers apart from each other. The area formerly known as Palestine by some, and Israel by others, was now a world park and cultural and historical preserve administered by UNESCO. Many of these areas had shown unusual and striking success, as people who had been struggling just to survive suddenly had a chance to thrive, like a plant that was dying in a darkened basement suddenly transplanted into the light of the great outdoors, spreading its leaves and reaching to the sky.

Most of the towns and farms in the vicinity of the lakes, however, were first come, first served, and each one blended the diverse elements of the worldwide human population in its own individual way. It turned out to be, in most cases, a very beautiful thing.

The technology wasn't complicated, it was mostly digging, and large amounts of explosives were used. It required a large work force but finding that was no problem at all and that part of the plan was realized quicker than anybody had dreamed possible.

Chapter 14

You keep on learning and learning, and pretty soon you learn something no one has learned before"

Richard Feynman

It was a perfect afternoon on campus, the brown leaves were blown across the lawns and the sidewalks. Dan was walking across the central lawn, briskly, which was in tune with the weather, but not running. His next class was statistics, which was easy for him, but it was an elective, so most of the kids in the class were pretty good. Still, if he was five minutes late it would not likely be remarked on and if it was, he could always say he was delayed in Drama class, which happened often enough to be believable, but wasn't actually true.

He enjoyed Drama, but you could see which kids were going to go on and make lives and careers out of it, and he wasn't one of them. Same with sports. Although he was much buffer than he'd been a couple of years ago, and a full eight centimeters taller, which could just be put down to a teenage growth spurt but Dan thought the cross country running had something to do with it, and the two hours in the gym each day lifting weights had given him a body that women did not find at all displeasing, he knew perfectly well he wasn't going to be a career athlete.

For a while he'd thought he might go into Law, but then Jason, his housemate and closest friend, had pointed out that he'd been watching too many old-timey, pre-transition films, which made it look like a dramatic and glamourous profession.

Now, AI sorted a lot of the minor cases and in a major criminal trial the emphasis had shifted from prosecution v. defense to an investigation which would actually determine the truth. Also, there just wasn't much crime anymore, as everybody had a decent life without it.

So, it was probably going to be mathematics. The ISP (International Space Program) was always looking for mathematicians, as were most large corporations, and government departments. And there was always teaching.

Of course, he could have done that just by staying in public school in Wackturtle Bay and going anywhere to college after that, but he was so incredibly glad he hadn't.

They say that all the cells in your body regenerate every seven years, and skin cells in like a few weeks, so in one way of looking at it, nobody was even the same person they were born as. Dan did not have such a poetic mind. While he was changed in many ways, he still felt that he was the shy nerd he'd always been, just one who'd learned a few tricks for keeping a conversation going. But, he had learned them very well.

After the day of the welcoming assembly, he'd been a bit miffed at his parents, and his school guidance counselor, but he had quickly come to realize that they were right. Almost everybody had.

He'd been back to Wackturtle Bay a few times, on vacation, but it was more just being a dutiful son than anything else. It wasn't calling him. He had no intention of living there as an adult.

Chapter 15

Everything had been leading up to this day. Her eighteenth birthday had been two weeks ago and she had enough credits to graduate early, but she stayed for the graduation ceremony at her parents insistence, and because she was valedictorian. That had been last night, she'd left the after party early, and at 7:45 a.m. she was on a train, which was now gliding smoothly across Texas, on her way to Iowa City, a place of lush midwestern greenery, a city which existed to serve its university.

She'd made arrangements on-line, so she knew that there was a job (as a waitress) and an apartment waiting for her. She'd be sharing the apartment with three other girls which, again, was an appeasement to her parents, sort of.

She agreed that it would be less complicated, and she had time for all that other stuff.

Chapter 16

Once upon a time, the parts of the body were having an argument about who should be the boss. The brain said it should be, of course, because it made all the decisions, even telling the other parts of the body when they should move.

The heart said it was the most important part because it pumped the blood to the brain, and everywhere else, so it should be the boss.

The lungs pointed out that without them, the body couldn't breathe and would soon die, the legs that the body couldn't go anywhere without them, the eyes that the body couldn't see where it was going without them, the mouth that they would all starve to death, and so on. The asshole was a bit tired of the argument, so it just closed up. Soon, the rest of the body began to feel uncomfortable.

The eyes watered, the mouth was clenching its teeth, and the brain got dizzy and was about to lose consciousness when they all decided to surrender and let the asshole be the boss. This proves that you don't need brains to be a boss. You just need to be an asshole.

Todd loved that old joke, or fable, or parable, or whatever the hell you wanted to call it. But, everybody in the recycling industry had heard it a million times, so he hadn't included it in the speech he'd just delivered to the World Recycling Convention, which had been, to his mind, a resounding success.

Now he was seated at an outdoor café on the Grand Boulevard of a gleaming, new, state of the art metropolis, enjoying a giant cheeseburger with fries and a glass of red wine, and checking his phone obsessively while he watched the crowds go by. He wasn't a big people watcher, had never liked people very much. "Look at them," he thought to himself. "They go through life, with their petty concerns, and have no idea what goes into making this world what it is."

The city gleamed. It was like a beam of sunlight on snow, like the starring tooth in a toothpaste commercial. The combination of sunlight, steel, glass, and water from all the fountains, everything reflecting every other thing, led to an impression of brightness that was almost overwhelming.

The trams were almost constant, within a minute of each other, shuttling up and down the concourse, and all the people walking by were beautiful and well dressed.

He was waiting for news from his plant. He had been a project manager for years, and now that Dickwad Corey, as Todd always referred to him (he was not the only one), was finally retiring, the position of plant superintendent was available. He was the logical choice, knew more about each aspect of the operation than anybody, and had initiated the garden program, although Corey had always taken credit for it.

Tired of watching the beautiful people walk by, he decided to check in on the plant's website. And there it was, staring him right in the face. Not only hadn't he got the job, he had no idea who this guy was who had. They'd hired somebody from the outside. He wasn't just disappointed. He was offended, he was outraged. It was an indicator that they hadn't even considered him for the job, that they'd rather have literally anybody else.

So, he quit. There was no reason to stay at a place that disrespected him like that. None at all.

Chapter 17

The future's always coming up
the past is always gone
even in Utopia
folks keep moving on

Olive's life had changed dramatically when she walked in on her husband having a weirdly scripted orgy in their marital bedroom that fateful day, but so had the lives of everyone involved.

Divorce was easy, because it was specifically stated in the new constitution that relations between people were none of the government's business, marriage was just a convenience between two consenting adults and either one could end it at any time with a simple request. Division of property could be a bit stickier, but in this case Olive had held all the cards. She got full custody, she got the house, and that's all she really needed. Outside of that, she'd been fairly generous, financially, and it was all settled quickly.

Roger had moved far away and got a job with a film production company in Berlin. Blondie had gone with him, but had soon moved on to bigger players, and better parts. He still saw the kids, like once or twice a year, which was enough, both for him and for them. Olive had eventually married Kirby, because he was always there anyway, and no other man could get close to her because of her level of fame and her dedication to her work and her children. Also, there was a bit of generalized distrust on her part with regard to Y chromosomed individuals.

The kids got along with him O.K. They didn't call him Dad and he didn't expect them to, but he made their mother happy, and they appreciated that. Olive had kept her name, just as she had with her first marriage. It was the name she was known by, and being known was very important to her. It was also her tag line, her catch phrase. Everybody in East Africa knew "Oh oh, here comes O. O." and would shout it out when they saw her walking down the street.

It just seemed like a logical progression. He was always at the house, eventually they started sleeping together because neither had anybody else, and then they got married. Which was televised, of course.

Martha had gotten another job as a nanny for a wealthy Asian family, but then left that for a job as a receptionist at the husband's firm. She was quite happily married to a local man, a plumber, and they had a comfortable flat and a newborn baby. The third girl in the trio had disappeared from the face of the Earth, as far as any of our principal players knew, but she was working as a bartender and sometimes tennis coach, in a city on another continent, thousands of kilometers away.

Everybody had put the incident behind them, and Olive had eventually erased the tape.

Chapter 18

I tip my hat to the new constitution
                              The Who

That government is best which governs least
                              Thomas Jefferson

Politicians are all crooks
and useless, by and large
it's time to put the scientists
and engineers in charge

Most people in Utopia agreed the UC, i.e Utopian Constitution, was a very fine and noble document, venerable even. Some said it was a fine work of literature, legal scholars pointed out that was a well-researched, lock down, rock solid document with very little ambiguity, very few loopholes, and even those loopholes (aka exemptions and special conditions) were tightly defined.

Its greatness lay not in the fact that it said what the administration* should do, stuff about stewarding the planet, creating a finer civilization and making life better for everybody, but in being very specific about what the administration could not do. The administration could not harm anybody, which meant war, of course, was totally out of the question, as was capital punishment, and even corporal punishment.

The administration could have nothing to do with religion, or any cultural thing like sports or movies or music or art, except of course for in schools. This meant no using public funds to buy sports stadiums for billionaires, and no special tax breaks for churches or church schools, but it also meant no artist grants, which angered some people on the left, but the greatest artist grant of all was guaranteed food and housing. Even a bad artist could live on that, and the good ones had all the time in the world to churn out good art.

They were allowed to manipulate the economy a bit, price caps on important items, printing more money as need be, issuing bonds, stuff like that, but they weren't allowed to use public funds to help specific companies, so no corporate bailouts or tax breaks, even though taxes weren't much of an issue any more. The administration had its own sources of income.

The administration was not allowed to legislate what people could or could not think, say, eat, or wear, who they could know, or love, or where they could go, or live. That was one of the greatest impositions on individual freedom that had been an ingrained part of society for the couple of thousand years preceding the transition, that people had been confined to small sections of the planet where they'd been born, their 'state,' their 'nation,' and not been allowed to freely roam, to amble, to wander, to travel anywhere across the surface of the big, beautiful planet which was their home.

Most importantly, perhaps, the administration was not allowed to keep things secret. When the Founder AI had written the plan, it had examined everything from all the computers of the world, and the world's governments were not excepted-their encryptions and codes were broken, their secrets examined and the AI had determined that the vast majority of what the world's governments were keeping secret was criminal, or very incriminating information about figures in public life, or evidence of corruption, skullduggery or flat out incompetence. Some was their secret plans to screw up other governments. A certain percentage was stuff that was just labeled secret for no reason at all, except habit.

The amount of stuff they were keeping secret because there was a valid reason for keeping it secret was so small that it made sense to just not allow the new administration to keep any secrets at all. And thus, the era of truth began.

That was critically important because, even though war was rendered obsolete with a one-world administration, there was an even greater risk of that one administration turning into a rigid, oppressive dictatorship.

So, some safeguards had to be taken to keep that big government small. Big enough to be efficient, sure, to make sure the trains ran on time, the water was kept drinkable, the hospitals clean, modern, and fully staffed, stuff like that, but small enough they couldn't interfere with individual rights or the traditions and ways of life in small communities. That was accomplished partly by having many different levels of power. The individual, of course, is and always has been the main unit and basis of our species. All the hopes and dreams we have in common are contained within each individual. Each individual, therefore, has the right, and the power to determine their own destiny.

Problems that couldn't be solved at the personal level perhaps could be solved at the friends and family level, above that was the community, and each community could set its own standards, as long as they didn't violate basic human rights. Each individual had the right to accept them, or to leave. Above the community, there were the regional administrations, over a thousand of them. The largest nations, which were the biggest threat to world peace, had been subdivided. A few had been combined, for convenience. Ireland, for example, and Korea. Many new homelands had been created on land that had formerly been barren desert. Everyone could go anywhere, and everybody had places where they would be welcome.

Another guarantee that government would not become too omniscient and oppressive was the independence of the main systems. The power and water grids of the planet were mainly operated by algorithm and were the main source of the global administration's wealth, but their human component was a meritocracy, and their leadership chosen from within. This was also true of the education system, the health system, the justice system, the waste disposal system, and the transportation system.

To calibrate the checks and balances even more finely, because history has shown us that corruption is almost inevitable, each of these bodies had a corresponding watchdog body, independent of them and charged with keeping them in line, focused on the greater good. People who worked there tended to be annoying, persnickety people, killjoys and bureaucrats, but they served an important role and were sought after, valued, and paid reasonably well.

Each department also had public liaison officers, who were there to help any time somebody had to deal with one of the different departments. They could get your kids into the most appropriate schools, or help you plan a trip to one of the world parks or help you to get a business license.

Then there was the Council of Experts, which most people called the Robot Congress because they used AI to figure out how to solve all human problems, and then edited the results so it wasn't something ridiculous. The human component of the Council of Experts was made up of scientists from numerous different fields, mathematicians and experts in economics, oceanographers, and agriculturalists, altogether a few thousand people, appointed by the governing bodies of their field of expertise, and working on a voluntary basis.

It was, admittedly, a rather large bureaucracy, but an extremely efficient one, and most people could get through their whole lives and never deal with the administration at all.

*The UC always referred to it as 'the administration' and not 'the government.' The logic was simple. A government governs. Top down. There is implied control, and a loss of individual freedom. An administration just administers. That is much less invasive.

Chapter 19

Even in a utopian world
of luxury and fun
there will still be work to do
and jobs that must be done

Veronika was in the middle of her freshman year and was doing pretty well in her studies. In a way, it was similar to High School, in that a lot of the kids were just coasting. On the one hand, this meant she was able to stay comfortably near the top of her classes without working too hard. On the other hand, she'd expected college to be, like, a higher level.

She didn't hate her job, as a waitress at Weird Willie's, which was somewhere between a burger joint and a family restaurant. She'd been waitressing since she was 16, baby-sitting since she was 12, so the work didn't faze her. They had decent food, reasonably priced, and the waitresses wore cute, little farm girl uniforms which looked absolutely nothing like anybody on a farm would actually wear—more like Dorothy from the Wizard of Oz or Mary Ann from Gilligan's Island – sexy, but not slutty, and impeccably cleaned and pressed. The meals were reasonably priced, but they also served beer and were not far at all off campus.

She didn't love it, either. She was making enough to live on, but living expenses were higher than they thought she would be, and the pay a bit less. She made 20 stacks an hour, but most people didn't tip much anymore, anywhere, because waitresses and waiters made enough to live on, and the prices were high enough.

Her plan (to graduate from college with a business degree and make a million stacks before she was 30) was still on track, but the train wasn't going very fast.

It had been a rough day. She'd woken up with a bit of a hangover and her classes had given her no respite. Then, they'd been pretty busy through the first few hours. She'd had a lot of coffee, managed to refrain from actually arguing with any customers, and got through the worst of it, but she was looking forward to 9 p.m. The restaurant was open to 11 but her study group came in at 9 and she had an agreement with her boss that she could join them as long as she got back up and waitressed whenever, you know, there were customers, and it meant she stayed to clean up and close at the end of the night, which didn't take long.

Jennifer and Robin came in a couple of minutes after nine. Veronika brought them a carafe of wine and a huge bucket of fries, their usual order, and sat down to join them. Roberta from Brooklyn, who told everybody she was going to be a great writer someday, but they'd all seen her poetry and knew otherwise, and Dani and Rose who may or may not have been a couple, came in together about 10 minutes later.

"Is this it?" Veronika (who most people called Ronnie now – it was shorter, they thought it was cute, and she really didn't mind) said. "Where are the guys?"

"Some sports thing," Dani said, with obvious contempt.

"Honestly, I think a couple of them aren't going to make it past the first year," Rose added.

"It's fine by me," Roberta said. "I really need to concentrate. I'm not so sure I'm going to pass, myself."

But, like always happened with the study group, they'd study a bit and then veer off into personal matters more often than not.

After about an hour they'd gone through a few carafes of wine, and after Veronika'd left the table to wait on customers for the fourth or fifth time, Robin leaned over to her and said "I know a job where you could make a lot more money for a lot less work."

"I'm listening," she said.

"Well," she said, and then "No, never mind."

"Oh, come on, you can't say something like that and then say 'never mind'"

"Maybe I'll just tell you later."

"Uh-uh, no way, no secrets in the sisterhood."

"What, maybe this is something we all could get in on."

"The mystery deepens"

Everybody had a comment, and Robin was sorry she'd opened her mouth. She really didn't want this to be public knowledge. It might change how people looked at her, and she rather liked things the way they were.

"O.K., she said. "but this does not leave the table."

(She'd be surprised if it didn't but it was too late now, these were, after all, her friends, and she was a little bit drunk.)

"I've been working a job on the weekends which pays pretty well, but it's not for everybody. Sex work."

"I never would have guessed that."

"Oh, wow"

"Where?"

"How much do you make?"

"Is it just dudes, or do you have sex with women, too?"

Again, everybody was talking at once.

"So, Ronnie, what do you think?" Jennifer asked, since the offer was to her.

"That.... would be a huge step. I've never even had sex at all yet."

This was a bigger bombshell than Robin's original suggestion.

"Whaaa..?"

"Like, what are you waiting for, girl. It's not like you don't have offers."

"Guys will pay extra for that, you know."

"We need more wine."

"I'll get it."

"You sit down!" came from six voices at once.

"Oh, Bobby, sweetheart, could you be a dear and bring us another carafe of your delightful house red."

Veronika was a bit impressed that Jennifer even knew the name of the young man (just 16, and earning a little pocket change, he was also the son of the owners) who was cleaning up tables and trying not to stare directly at the table. In his eyes, they were all gorgeous, but he'd become a bit obsessed with Ronnie ever since she'd started working there. He didn't have to be here this late at night. He chose to.

"No problem, coming right up."

They carried on drinking, and talking, and Robin was relieved, not that she expected them to keep mum forever, but none of them had totally freaked over it, so maybe nobody would be compelled to make a big deal over it.

The guys from the study group came in, as a unit, around 10:30, and the conversation crashed to a halt and all of a sudden they were engrossed on a question in one of their textbooks. It would have been obvious, if the guys were at all observant, but they weren't, particularly. They got in a round of drinks, and then left, with five of the six girls and a promise from Veronika to meet up with them later, but she was lying.

She helped Bobby with the final cleanup and, on their way out the door, said "How would you like to come home with me and have sex?"

Chapter 20

How many deaths will it take till we know
that too many people have died
                    Bob Dylan "Blowin' in the Wind"

If you say it's a lovely day
there are those who will object
it's their nature, it's their way
it's automatic, I suspect
We could have a better world
Utopia, a paradise
though there are those who would object
I think it would be rather nice

Once the transition was complete, the results were dramatic and today, people wonder why it took two decades instead of two years, or even one, because logistically it could have been, but people tended to forget how fierce the opposition had been. The wealthy, the owners of corporations, and factories, who employed billions, screamed bitterly about the expense, and how paying higher wages would bankrupt them and destroy the economy, but their real worry, which they seldom said out loud, was that if there were no poverty nobody would be forced to work for them at substandard wages in horrible conditions, they would not be able to get anybody to work for them. Both objections, in the end, turned out to be spurious. Some invested in mechanization and robotics, others bit the bullet and paid higher wages, some did go out of business, but it didn't destroy their lives and others were there to take their place. The Everybody Gets a Job program, which did, indeed, require a huge initial expenditure, showed some results almost immediately. Since a lot of money was flowing to people who had almost no money, it was mostly spent on food, and clothing, and lots of other cheap and basic things which meant an infusion of cash into the economy at the base, and it started to trickle up. The construction of the worldwide water grid and the coastal redevelopment program meant that the first hurricane season was less damaging than the last pre-transition one, and the first forest fire season as well. The first long, hot summer after the transition showed a dramatic drop in the crime rate, especially in places with the highest, most violent crime rates, because those areas, aka the slums of the world's largest cities, had been purged of their most violent demographic. Almost every male between the ages of 18 and 30 was working for eight hours every day (or pursuing higher education), and most of them were out of town.

A secondary wave hit a couple of years in, as completely new, built from the ground up, environmentally self-sustaining cities absorbed a great deal of the population, and provided employment as well. The base wage the world government was paying became a de facto minimum wage, as nobody had any incentive to work in the private sector unless they were topping it. A lot of the people in the Everybody Gets a Job program were starting to move into homes they'd worked on themselves. And the world government was starting to take in revenue from the world energy grid and the world water grid. Even though the rates were so low even the poorest could pay them, there were billions of rate payers. Billions of pennies meant hundreds of millions of stacks. As the farms around the newly created lakes reaped their first harvest, they began to pay for themselves, and huge zones of prosperity spread across the Earth. Food prices even began to drop a bit.

The airlines had complained bitterly that they were losing money to the railroads, and the zeppelins. They'd had to scale down and consolidate, they were now pretty much only used for trans-oceanic travel, but they were still all making a nice profit off businesspeople in a hurry and rich people who didn't care. The railroads, which were forced by law to carry people for free, still made money by establishing a luxury class, a business class, and a very affordable economy class, and only in the last few cars did the poor people have to sit in seats which didn't conform to their body shape, and get through the whole journey without the benefit of stewards and stewardesses (most of whom were young people, ready to accept a basic minimum wage for the great perk of seeing the world). Also, the railroads made a great deal of money on freight, while still being cheaper than trucks had been.

The rich complained that the poor were getting handouts and there was no incentive to work anymore, and yet people continued to work, certainly enough of them to keep everything running. People still became teachers because they wanted to teach, and doctors and nurses still became doctors and nurses, because they wanted to heal the sick, and some people still became farmers, because they loved being in touch with the Earth and seeing things grow and, now that power and water were cheap and unlimited, and expert advice, of course, was free, farming was a pretty sweet gig.

The complaints did die down eventually, except among the cruelest, most reactionary and most perverted one percent among the one percent who truly loved making poor people suffer, because the rich were getting the biggest handout of all -the privilege of remaining rich – which turned out to be even better when nobody was poor. After a night at the opera, or a glitzy, expensive art auction, men in tuxedoes and women in evening gowns could stroll the streets of even the largest city by night, without any fear of street crime.

Solving the problem of poverty, surprisingly, turned out to be much easier than solving the problem of war.   Before the transition, many people actually thought of war as a necessary part of human civilization, necessary for the economy and technological development, necessary for each nation to survive the relentless onslaughts of all the others. It had always been, therefore people were resigned to it always being, and it didn't help that the world's largest governments were essentially owned by people who loved war, who profited from war, and maintained their power by controlling the media, and manipulating elections. It had to start with baby steps, and even those baby steps were only possible after the U.N. was reformed, so the major powers no longer had an inviolable veto.

Baby step number one was the military tax. In the first year, all nations had to donate to the world government 1% of whatever they'd spent that year on their military, for building hospitals and schools and good stuff like that. In the 2nd year it was 2%, in the 3rd year, 3 percent, and onward. Countries with large military expenditures could either pay up or become a little less heavily armed, and either way was a win for the world at large.

Baby step number two was the de-escalation from attack position initiative (DEFAP), which said that any nation which had military bases in a different country had to convert them into something that would benefit the local populace. This mostly concerned the former United States of America, which had over 750 such bases, more than any other country by at least 700. Many were converted into schools, which was not difficult as they already had water and sanitation facilities, kitchens, and buildings which could be classrooms. Guantanamo Bay in Cuba was now a very busy port and a major tourist destination, a land of beaches, music and rum, with a small memorial commemorating the horrors that had gone on in the torture prison there, late in the pre-transition period.

Baby step number three was the global coast guard, which was meant as more of a police force than a military unit, and it recruited primarily jobless people, an equal mix of men and women, from impoverished lands. Neither being jobless nor the happenstance of having been born in an economically deprived political division of the planet was a requirement, of course, but it did work out that way.

Their job was rescue at sea, which was less problematic now in a world without borders because there weren't any crowded, leaky boats full of refugees, protecting the shipping lanes from pirates, who pretty much had disappeared from existence with the Everybody Gets a Job program, and making it unnecessary for any nation to have a navy, which had been a big problem at the beginning of the transition because the larger sovereign nations had very much wanted to keep their independent navies, and use them to blockade smaller nations who, for some reason unfathomable to modern historians (the general consensus being that it had always been bullshit, and the biggest mystery was how they had sold it to their people) they "felt" were a threat to them. Baby step number four was a whole bunch of co-operative inter-national programs. The largest of those was bringing the world's scientists and engineers together to create the Earth Space Program, based in Kazakhstan but with launch pads, observation stations, landing strips and research centers all over the world, and a group of scientists who were far more dedicated to space research than any particular nation.

Baby step number five was The People's Peace Conference, which was basically an online forum but wound up producing some great ideas.

None of these, however, were as important to the creation of world peace as was the overall new social order.

The complete elimination of poverty, hunger and homelessness left people much less to fight over, unlimited peacetime job opportunities meant a lot fewer people signing up for war, and the international public transportation system and people being allowed to go, and live, and work anywhere on Earth they wanted to, meant that even the most warlike people had no place to aim their evil intent, because some of their people were likely to be living there.

War was done and a new era of peace and prosperity for all mankind had been ushered in.

It was amazing how quickly most people came to take the new reality for granted. Within 20 years, there were millions of college graduates who didn't even remember the old world. Within 40 years, anybody who remembered the old times, waved the old flags, and talked, passionately, about ancient conflicts was considered a doddering old fool.

Nobody worried about the fact that most decisions were being made by AI programs, and the human government was a rubber stamp. They continued to vote, or not, and celebrated when their favorite candidates won, and complained when anybody else did, but carried on with their lives. It was not the end of the world.

They were not dancing in the streets and celebrating the tremendous progress humankind had made. If they now owned their own home, which they never had before, they attributed it to their own perseverance and hard work, or maybe just to good luck and being quick to seize on the opportunity.

A very few bitter philosophers complained about how ease was corrupting the people and making us all weak, but nobody paid much attention to them.

Life was good. Life is supposed to be good.

Chapter 21

Ronnie had decided to give it a shot. Most of the girls took fake names, just a long-standing tradition and she thought it prudent, since she wasn't sure she wanted this job, this lifestyle, this lifestyle as a job, this job as a lifestyle. So, she called herself Charlotte, because that sounded sexy and not like her own name at all.

She worked a weekend – the place was a Mississippi river boat, a short train ride from campus, long enough to do a bit of homework, read a couple chapters, or just relax and enjoy the countryside - telling her bosses at Willie's that she was just going away for the weekend, and they didn't press for details. They liked her, but they could replace her easily enough.

She was surprised to find she didn't mind the job at all, she rather enjoyed it and felt no moral qualms whatsoever – the only part she didn't like was the costume, she'd traded one hokey male fantasy themed uniform for another, equally unrealistic one. No southern belle had ever worn anything quite so – revealing.

She quit waitressing, gave notice on Monday and began working every weekend, then she worked through most of the summer, only going home for a couple of weeks, then she arranged her sophomore class schedule so she only had morning classes and began working every day. She enjoyed it, and she loved the money she was making. Her plan to make a million before she was 30 was back on the fast track, even if it was a very different track.

Her major was in business, but by the end of her sophomore year, she'd come up with an idea for her own business, an employee–owned chain of brothels.

A degree in business seemed superfluous after that, so she changed her major to psychology, figuring that was what would help her the most in her new endeavor. She was not wrong.

Chapter 22

It was a cozy, family scene in the living room of Olive Odhiambo's mansion. There was her and Kirby, the three kids, and her campaign manager, who was also her PR person at the show. It had been her producer's idea that she run for president, as a ratings ploy, but she was insistent that if she was going to be in the race, she was not going to treat it as a joke. She felt that would be disrespectful, and maybe even harmful, and she wouldn't be a party to that.

So, here they were. Her campaign manager, Shirley Adams, had made up a bunch of cards with questions on them and her, Kirby, and the kids were taking turns asking them. They had snacks, they had drinks. It was like a family game night and she was enjoying herself thoroughly.

"Everybody knows the seven priorities," her daughter Rachel, now 14, a smart but somewhat lazy student who dreamed of being a singer, read. "Why, in your opinion, is saving the planet prioritized above the preservation of the human race?"

"There are a couple of reasons, actually." Olive had a planned response for every one of the cards. The key in the upcoming debate would be memorizing them, and knowing enough about policy, history, science, and world politics to ad lib a response in the not at all unlikely event something that wasn't foreseen would be asked. O.K., two keys.

"First, of course, the survival of our planetary ecosystem is a prerequisite for the survival of our species, so it makes a lot of sense. Second, most individuals, at least most normally sane adult individuals, are pretty good at taking care of their own survival and 90% of what they need from government is to leave them alone." Kirby was nodding enthusiastically at that line. He didn't necessarily think it true, but it never hurt a politician to present themselves as anti-government. "But third, and I think this is very important" she paused a bit, and took a sip of wine, before leaning forward a bit – despite the intimacy of the gathering, she was already practicing for the cameras – "it gives us a sense of humility. Not many people are alive today who remember the times before the transition, but my mother is one of them, and as she's told me many times, and my children, that we almost destroyed the planet before The Plan was implemented. There were terrible floods, and wildfires. Lots of species went extinct. Still, there were those so arrogant that they thought mankind should have total dominance over the planet. There are still people like that, but we can never allow them to have that kind of power again."

Her campaign manager was exultant. She'd brought in not only her kids but her mother, it was a multi-generational trifecta, the response would satisfy both the environmentalists and the small government crowd, who were generally not even close to each other on the political spectrum, and she looked calm and natural, yet quietly assertive when doing it. An iron fist in a velvet glove. That wasn't the campaign slogan or anything, it's just how Shirley envisioned her. She didn't say anything, she didn't want to micromanage the practice session, and she certainly didn't want to interrupt the candidate when she was doing great. Instead, she just said "O.K., Bob, it's your turn."

Robert, the middle child, was now 11, and he was the quiet one. Unnervingly quiet, sometimes. "There's a lot of debate about big government vs. small government. Where do you stand on that?" This was a trap question, and almost guaranteed to come up at the debates. "The question isn't big government or small government. The question is good government." She held up a finger, to forestall Shirley's objection. "Maybe that sounds a bit too glib," she continued. "Let me elaborate. We need a big enough government, enough of a socialist economy, to guarantee that everybody on Earth has a decent home with hot and cold running water, electricity, the basic comforts. Everybody should have access to state-of-the-art health care, for free, health care is a right, and the same goes for a good education. These are not just the things individuals need, they will make our society stronger and more productive overall. The government, on the other hand, needs to be small enough that it doesn't interfere with people's personal lives. I am against the government getting involved in religion, or culture, or sports, or even the free flow of the economy, although a few safeguards might be necessary." This not only sounded good, it was constitutionally unassailable. The constitution, in fact, said exactly that, although it took several pages to say it, with listings of exceptions, addenda, and details.

They went around the circle a few more times, little Charlie sometimes stumbling over the big words and sometimes not understanding the question at all. Occasionally they would discuss her answers afterwards, changing a word or two here and there. After an hour or so it was almost time for the kids to pack it in when once more it was Charlie's turn. He looked at the card, pretending to read it, and said "If you're elected president, will you let your children get a puppy?" That card hadn't been in the deck, but actually Shirley had to admit it was the kind of question they were likely to ask.

"Well, Clare" Olive said, looking directly at Charlie. Clare Park of the BBC would likely be one of the moderators, and she was famous for questions like this. Charlie understood the joke just fine. "I am, of course, a big believer in teaching children responsibility. If the kids would promise to take care of the dog, take him for walks, bathe

him, and always do their homework, I suppose I
would consider it."

Chapter 23

At first, he had just been her accountant. They say you should never sleep with anybody you work with, and that's usually good advice, except when it's not. He had helped her diversify her business, and her goal of becoming a millionaire by the time she was 30 had been accomplished by the time she was 28. They were about the same age, both very attractive people, and seemed to be interested in the same things, the most important of which was making her a boatload of money. Also, most men were intimidated by her. Dan, refreshingly for her, was not.

Her employee-owned brothel was still the heart of her business, with locations all over North America, but she now also owned, in whole or in part, a chain of beauty salons and a chain of fitness centers, both of which gave sizable discounts to her girls, a luxury resort in Uruguay, a house cleaning service, a chain of donut shops, a talent agency, and a line of cosmetics.

Then came a perfect, warm, full moon evening after they'd been dating and working together for a couple of years. They were at an outdoor café along the banks of the Los Angeles river, a very romantic spot which attracted tourists from all over the world, which was a bit ironic because Los Angeles had lost about 3/4ths of its population in the transition. The river buses, lit up like Christmas trees, stopped at almost every café to drop some people off and pick other people up. There were no set stops, just wherever people asked, or wherever people were waiting.

It wasn't quite an official, one knee type of proposal, but he did mention the possibility of marriage, and clearly indicated he'd be in favor of it. She hadn't said yes, exactly. Marriage had never been part of her plan, and she was happy with the relationship the way it was. They talked about it, both as a romance (she was a trained psychologist, after all) and from a practical standpoint (he couldn't stop being an accountant), all the different aspects; where would they live, pre-nup or no pre-nup (he'd readily agreed to one – she had way more money than him, and the gap was widening every day, but she was paying him a very good salary, plus stock options, bonuses, and some benefits.

Besides, he wasn't as concerned with money as she was. He just happened to be very good at it), whether to have kids (he wanted them more than she did, but neither of them were in a frantic hurry), who would take whose last name, and in the end decided to take a trip around the world together, a year, maybe two, and if they were still in love after all that, she'd marry him.

Chapter 24

Todd was still seething. He had taken a job at a different recycling center, halfway around the world from Corey Gardens, as it was now called. His idea, which he had thought of as a nice blending of recycling and gardening, had actually turned out to be much more, the beginning of the idea that recycling centers should recycle themselves, and become beautiful, elaborate gardens, or very productive farms.

He had gotten zero credit for it, zero recognition, and zero profit. He wasn't going to make that mistake again. He'd used his savings to buy himself a truck, a house and a small plot of land not far from his job, taken a welding course in his spare time, and focused on what he considered the second great idea of his lifetime, making art from garbage.

His neighbors weren't thrilled about it, but they didn't live that close, he'd planted big hedges all around, they didn't have any legal grounds to stop him, and he didn't like them much anyway.

Chapter 25

Of all the contestants, Olive Odhiambo was beginning to realize, she had an advantage. With her background in television, she was used to all this – the lights, the microphones, the studio audience. Also, since she hadn't expected to get this far, and certainly didn't expect to win, she was under less pressure than a lot of them. She had a bit of a following from her days as the host of 'Good Morning, Nairobi,' but she was virtually unknown outside Africa and had never been elected to anything. She wasn't the only one in the running of whom that last thing could be said.

Yet, here she was, along with eleven other candidates, in the final debates before the election for President of the World.

Of course, she hadn't been too surprised to get through the preliminary rounds. That's when the

130

crazies were eliminated.*

There was the guy who believed there should be public hot tubs everywhere, saying that this was a way of building communities, who also went on a somewhat overly enthusiastic rant about the joys of nudity, which made even the most ardent social liberals in the viewing audience a bit nervous; the guy who wanted to have a social credit rating system and anybody who didn't get above a minimum score would be put into a multi-generational ark ship and sent to the nearest star likely to have a habitable planet; the woman who was obsessed with putting public toilets at every bus stop; and the architect who had an extreme and passionate hatred of graffiti. While the other candidates had got quite a bit of mileage out of mocking them, Olive had just stuck to her message, which was "I'll have a transparent administration." Even when the other candidates took to social media following the debate to hammer the less relevant candidates, she took a gentler tone and issued a statement to say that "While these candidates may have gotten carried away with specific issues, they weren't completely wrong.

I'm not against hot tubs or public toilets, and I'm certainly not against space exploration or pro-graffiti. But, if I should be elected, my priority would be fighting corruption, strengthening the bonds that have led to peace, and not spending too much money."

That was six debates ago, and the final twelve had had debates on topics ranging from ethics, humanity vs. the robots, individual rights as opposed to the community needs (Olive's position was as much individuality as possible, as much community as necessary, which made for a nice slogan but she was perfectly capable of elaborating, when asked), to how they would balance the job with their personal life.

Now, this was the final debate. She still didn't expect to win, she was 5th in the polls, but her attitude was not exactly the same as it had been when she was first nominated. She had noticed that all of the other candidates –every single one of them – tended to answer every question by quickly and expertly shifting back to their favorite topics and sound bites. It would, if they were doing it right, sound like they were addressing the topic, but they really weren't. 'It might be smart politics,' she thought, 'but it's not a good sign about how they will lead.' She still wasn't sure if she wanted the job, but she now felt she'd be able to do as good a job of it as any of them.

When the question "Once the infrastructure is completed, how are you going to find jobs for everyone?" was asked, all of the candidates, predictably, dismissed the question with some version of "We'll cross that bridge when we come to it" or "What a silly question, when we've completely achieved a utopian society, the only problem is keeping it going" before they segued back to their favorite talking point, which was usually their long experience and a very questionable list of their accomplishments.

Odhiambo, on the other hand, addressed the question, and talked about developing new fields, and training programs, and getting more people involved in science. She also talked about establishing a full time colony on Mars which, she admitted, would only employ a very few people, even counting the support team on Earth, and building an underground society, which would guarantee the survival of the human race in the event of a nuclear war, which wasn't entirely eliminated as a threat yet, or an asteroid strike or an EMP wave from a neutron star, and mean even faster train service in vacuum tubes with no obstructions. She was worried that maybe people would think she'd wandered into crazy territory, but she spoke clearly, and softly, and presented it all as a jobs program, so her answer turned out to be a popular one.

She came in third in the first round of voting, and nobody had a majority, so ranked-choice voting kicked in, and a lot of people had had her as their second choice. Within two hours of the polls closing, she was announced as the next president of Earth.

She was a bit stunned by the hugeness of it all, intimidated by the responsibility, and scared. But she smiled for the cameras, waved to the crowd, and started making plans for her administration.

*The real crazies were eliminated before the debates began. All candidates for President of Earth, and quite a few lower offices, had to pass a mental health exam, and also an IQ test (minimum score, 120). They also couldn't have a felony conviction on their record, but almost nobody had that anymore.

Chapter 26

It's a beautiful world we live in
DEVO

Dawn was breaking, outside the window, as the train floated, silently but at 400 kilometers per hour, across the broad, flat land. Fields of tall corn, fields of fat, dense marijuana bushes, fields of bright yellow sunflowers flashed by the window in seconds, although some of them were a couple kilometers long, and just as wide. The homes were like palaces on the prairie, although it wasn't really possible to get a good look.

Daniel de Leon wondered how much of this beauty, this magnificently lush bounty, was natural, and how much was due to human intervention. This is the world upon which we evolved, he thought. Therefore, we are suited to it in every way because we are a part of it. We could not have evolved anywhere else, and this planet could not have led to the existence of any other than ourselves. On the other hand, the native flora of this once dry land would have been much sparser.

He looked at the blonde goddess lying down next to him, covered with a light blue silk sheet, a black mask over her eyes and her seat reclined 45 degrees– and thought "I must be the luckiest guy in the world."

They'd started their round the world trip about 10 month ago, and were zipping westward across southern Siberia. Their relationship was better than ever. They'd had a few disagreements, of course. In Turkey, he'd gone out for a day touring an archaeological site while she'd just had a spa day, something they usually did together, but they'd still met up for dinner and they certainly didn't go to bed angry. There was the incident in Encatorce, when he'd suggested they buy all her mother's artwork to decorate their corporate headquarters, and she'd said he was doing it just to suck up to her parents, which he totally was, but it worked and her parents loved him, which she had to admit, in the end, was a good thing. They'd had a similar argument in Wackturtle Bay, as she was so taken with the town, and his parents, that she suggested they get a place there as a married couple, and she was astounded at the vehemence with which he rejected that suggestion. At the beginning of the trip, she'd wanted to always travel in first class, because it was first class and they had the money, but he'd argued for business, sometimes even for economy, because it was still very nice and the first class prices were truly ridiculous, but after a while she agreed with him that the difference in service between first and business was truly miniscule, and they almost always settled for business after that. He tended to be an early riser. She was a night owl. Minor stuff.

For the most part it had been a magnificent trip. They'd hiked in mountains, camped in the desert, and slept in luxury hotels. They'd taken a stroll along a wood and rope bridge through the rain forest canopy in Nicaragua and spent many hours sipping rum on tropical beaches. They'd stayed in picture perfect seaside villages, gone scuba diving on ancient shipwrecks, visited the great underwater dome off the coast of Belize, done ayahuasca in Peru, and stayed for about a week in a town where all the housing was high up on a hill and all the shops, schools, restaurants and businesses were down in the valley and every morning people would take the slides down the hill, and in the evening they'd come back up on the funicular. It had been a laugh at first, but it didn't have a big permanent population because people got tired of the novelty. Some stayed because the housing market was depressed, and it was fairly easy on a moderate income to turn two flats into one, and the funicular did work both ways. They'd traveled by airplane, zeppelin (appropriately luxurious, but not a big deal, they agreed), train, ship, camel, and a horse drawn caravan in Bulgaria, which they'd enjoyed very much, making love in the swaying box while they listened to the clip-clop of the horses' hooves, and the driver waving and calling out to passersby. They'd gone to Antarctica to see the penguins, experienced Mardi Gras in Rio and Dia do Los Muertes in a small town in Mexico (which was nothing new for Veronika). He'd learned to speak Spanish, which she spoke as well as English, of course, they'd both picked up a smattering of several languages, and felt very cosmopolitan indeed. They'd visited World World in Africa and spent over a month there, sampling as many of the cuisines of the world as they could. They enjoyed the sight and the scents of New Hanging Gardens of Babylon, and one place they particularly liked was a canal town where many of the balconies, in houses and hotels alike, were diving platforms, and people were just jumping and splashing all day long. They'd usually spend a few minutes in the evening checking on their business interests, and occasionally they'd make an investment along the way. She'd divested from the core of her business, because employee–owned meant employee owned, and it was a younger womens' game. She really liked the sound of saying that she was the CEO of an international conglomerate, though. They'd talked about marriage quite frequently and, without any formal proposal, they both agreed and understood that it was going to happen. "It's as if we're having the honeymoon first" she'd said one evening, as they were deliberately having their dessert before dinner, a coconut pecan baklava, with a regional white wine, as they sat on the terrace of their guesthouse and watched the sun going down across the Caspian sea, because that was a thing they sometimes did. He did not disagree.

Chapter 27

In her first week as President, Olive had realized that the answer she had given in the last debate, the answer that may have been responsible for her getting elected, was to be definitive of her administration. All the homes and schools were built, the rail network spanned the world, there were an adequate number of hospitals and clinics, and the Everybody Gets a Job program was, indeed, having trouble finding jobs for everybody. The retirement age was being gradually lowered, people had more vacation time than ever, the three-day weekend (staggered, not everybody could stop working at once, because the pubs and restaurants wanted to always be open) was becoming very common, and still the work force outweighed the work that needed to be done.

She wasn't too fazed, her experience as a talk show host had taught her how to think on her feet, and her plan, her strategy, was still just to listen to the best advice she could (which usually meant the so-called robot congress) and act on it.

She started digging. That is, she poured money

into putting railroads underground, vacuum tubes rather than magnetic levitation, even faster. At each station there were shops, and large areas were hollowed out. No matter what disaster would befall the human race in future, nuclear war or alien invasion, there would be shelter.

She also poured money into space, but the Martian colony was still small, a few scientists, not many of them willing to spend their whole lives there, it was smaller than the outposts in Antarctica, and enlarging it would take more than just manpower, more than money. So, she focused on the space elevator project, which would pave the way for big time exploration, regular fleets taking off for Mars every couple of years for a couple of months when the window came around, mining in the asteroid belt, space hotels, and maybe even some day, although this was still in the far future, the terraforming of Venus.

Most people didn't notice, but everybody that wanted a job had a job, the economy kept chugging along nicely, and her popularity rating stayed high. She'd have been a shoo-in for a second term, if she'd wanted one, which she didn't.

Chapter 28

They had decided the wedding was to take place at Bogatynia Tower. It was the largest building in the world, so that was something they could tell the grandkids. Built on the site of a pre-transition open pit coal mine, a hideously unsightly gash in the Earth, it went up to 110 stories, and there were an equivalent number below ground. At its base, it covered 30 square kilometers. There were a handful of giant buildings like this around the world, but they hadn't been as successful as foreseen. They had plenty of space for residences or businesses, but most of the pits were out in the middle of nowhere and it was much easier and made more economic sense just to flood them. Like trees and wild flowers, the world could not have too many lakes.

Bogatynia Tower had several different hotels, so they'd easily managed to reserve a section for all of their guests on the 54th floor, with spectacular views of the fairy tale farms and villages in Poland and Germany (from the south side of the building they could have looked down into Czechia) but that wasn't the main draw.

That was the grotto. It took up what would have been floors 35 to 45 below ground, which gave it a very high ceiling. It looked the Hall of the Mountain King or the courtyard of Khazad Dum in its days of golden glory, when there was free trade with elves, and men, and the occasional daring hobbit, when the great hall rang with the clang of hammers on steel and gold, and the chatter and laughter of all the happy folk. It appeared to be entirely carved out of natural stone (the framework of the building was discreetly hidden) and it contained, within its exquisitely twisted rock walls and linked by many a hidden staircase, restaurants, beer halls, wine bars, auditoriums where the world's leading talents routinely performed, an art school, hiking trails, several small souvenir ships taking advantage of the theme, and more than a few wedding halls. They'd booked one of those.

His parents had arrived by train, hers had flown in, along with her brother and sister, they'd saved up their UBI's for months and Ronnie and Dan were paying for everybody's accommodation. A lot of his friends from Rocklaw had come and, as it was not very far away, were making a bit of a class reunion out of it, and a few of his friends from university as well. Some of her college friends had made it, her old study group was all there, and a whole lot of her business associates.

It was not the world's biggest wedding, but it was a great one. Great quantities of food and alcohol were consumed, many happy tears were shed, the dancing lasted long into the night, and several new relationships were formed. Late the next afternoon, after a large post wedding breakfast buffet and a more intimate, just family post wedding lunch, our happy hero and heroine descended to a couple of levels below the magic cavern, to the vacuum tunnel train station, a work of art in its own right, with connections to Berlin, Prague and Warsaw in under half an hour, and Paris, Moscow, Rome or Istanbul in under two hours.

They went to Prague, still considered one of the most romantic cities on the planet, since this was officially their honeymoon. They toured the castle, had dinner in the garden at Letna Park, overlooking the river and all its bridges, walked around Old Town for a while and, in the dark stillness of night, walked across Charles Bridge, and looked at the swans bobbing on the still waters close to shore, like marshmallows on cocoa. There was no more romantic place in the world.

The next day they took a train to Paris, and a couple of days after that jetted back to their starting point. They still hadn't decided where home was to be, although they felt very at home anywhere in the world, but they had completed the circuit.

About a week after that, she informed him that she was two months pregnant. He'd thought, at the wedding, that he could not possibly be any happier. He was wrong.

Chapter 29

President Odhiambo arrived ten minutes early for the weekly meeting, which was not unusual, and as soon as she got there everybody else began to enter the room. It was as if they'd been waiting, which they had. Nobody wanted to be late, and when the President was in the room, even coming on time could be seen as late.

It was force of habit, really. This was to be the last meeting of her term, nobody's job was on the line, and the department heads' jobs were never on the line, as promotions for the various departments were all handled internally, in some cases on a points basis. Nonetheless, she was the boss, and everybody felt that very strongly.

"It looks like everybody's here, so let's begin. First, I'd like to say it's been a pleasure working with all of you, and I wish you all the best of luck in the future. Now, let's hear from transportation."

"We set a record last week. No train was off schedule by more than 30 seconds. Co-ordination between local transport systems and the international grid continues to improve. We added 600 kilometers of bike paths, using all recycled materials, with 14 new rest areas. The planes, the zeppelins, and the roads are largely out of our control, but I'm sorry to say, there was a road fatality last week. Some schmuck drove through a guard rail on a mountain road in Croatia."

"I heard about that. I take it an investigation is happening?"

"Of course. (It was actually during the previous administration that the Transportation Department had started treating automobile accidents like airline accidents – viewing each one as an opportunity for an investigation and viewing each investigation as an opportunity to improve safety features.) The family's calling it a tragic accident, the insurance company's calling it suicide. He was driving way too fast for that road, and he was hammered."

"How the hell did he start the car if he was drunk?"

"If you know enough about auto mechanics and computers, you can figure out a bypass."

"Well, it's a shame. Even in a perfect world, people are going to screw up."

"Yeah. Anyway, back in the good news category,

the trains in India are experimenting with 'culture cars,' which they also call 'tourist class.' Food, music, stewards in costumes, it's basically Bollywood on the rails. So far, it seems to be a hit."
"Yes, I've heard of that. Hope other regions pick it up. Let's hear from education."
"We're doing fine. The world population is holding steady, even starting to dip a bit, so we'll have no problem keeping class sizes under a dozen for the foreseeable future...."
"Foreseeable future?"
"The next five or ten years down the road, we haven't projected further than that."
"Well, I guess I'm covered then."
There were chuckles at that.
"Also, our research departments are making some major strides. Coming up with new stuff almost every day...."
"Such as?"
"I think we'll have a space elevator by the end of the decade."
"Well, damn, somebody else is going to get credit for that. (more chuckles) It'll send the economy through the roof when it happens. Environment?"

"The recycling program is humming away beautifully. It's almost all robotized now, including collection. Almost no plastics are reaching the ocean. Agriculture is doing well. A few reports of farmers using banned herbicides and pesticides, but the problem there is the local governments. They don't want to crack down on their own."

"Haven't we shut down the manufacturers?"

"We have, but there are people who've figured out how to produce this shit at home."

"Talk to justice."

"They've been informed."

"Good. Moving on. Justice?

They continued around the table like this, with reports from the Energy Department, the Water Department, the Future Planning Department, the Space Agency, and all the other departments. Mostly, Chairman Odhiambo just accepted the report, and only made suggestions sparingly. That's the way her administration had been run. She had taken advice from the so-called Robot Congress, and it had never once let her down. Her administration, she felt confident, would be remembered as a time when nothing significant happened, and people would mostly remember her weekly chats, which were quite popular.

Chapter 30

*In this world, there is room enough
we don't have to all like the same stuff*

Todd Katz was, by almost anybody's definition, a mean old coot, a buzzard, a crank, a curmudgeon, and his home reflected his personality. There was the stone cottage that had been there when he'd purchased the property, and that was like so many others in the region, light and breezy, the indoors not so completely separated from the outdoors. Most people left it at that and had beautiful gardens, farms, ponds, swimming pools and tennis courts around their plain and comfortable homes, but not Todd. Oh, no. He'd kept adding onto it over the years; A trailer here, a shipping crate there, steel beams welded together at odd angles, and long strands of wire woven between them, and lights from old derelict cars, hanging from those wires, which lit the whole place up in tangents of red and yellow light, which danced in the breeze when there was a breeze, wind chimes made of all sorts of tinkly garbage, and howling whistles made of pipes and tubes with holes drilled through them. It wound around the whole property and made for a bizarre and cacophonous sound and light show which the neighbors tended to think of as a demonic hellscape, and Todd thought was beautiful.

He called it The Dragon, they called it crap, a blight on the neighborhood. They'd taken him to court many times. Sometimes he won, sometimes they won. Under the World Constitution for a Utopian Society, people had tremendous leeway with what they did on their own property, but they had forced him to plant trees, tall trees, all around the property line. The alternative would have been to reduce the height of the structure, and he wasn't about to do that. They'd also forced him to submit to regular environmental inspections, but they'd failed in their attempts to have him declared insane, or to have the property seized.

At ground level there were planters made of tires and old refrigerators which were all filled with the same crazy blend of grass, weeds and wild flowers as the spaces between them, car and bus seats scattered around as lawn furniture, which mostly went unused as he never invited guests, and only occasionally tolerated them, walls made of recycled glass bottles and bits of stone and shell which weren't part of any buildings but just meandered aimlessly. There were windows which weren't associated with any walls, either hanging in the air or slotted into the ground. There were potted plants hanging from the structure above, so that the green hanging down from the sky and the green growing up from the ground almost met in high summer. Some called it Seussian, but the vast majority of his neighbors considered it the physical manifestation of an extremely disturbed mind.

He had an O.K. life. No friends, like, in the physical universe, but he did have a small online following, there were a few dozen people who'd seen photos of his convoluted creation and clicked the like button, a handful who had even commented. Also, there were a few ex-colleagues who didn't hate him, who had even done him favors over the years, and who would say hello if they ever met him in town, which didn't happen often because he seldom went into town.

He was quite proud of the work he'd done, how he'd risen from poverty and squalor up to home-owning, middle class squalor. Artist proud, even. He knew that his neighbors, and pretty much everybody within 50 kilometers, was just waiting for him to die. He didn't have any close family, and they figured the property would revert to the state and they could dismantle all his work and get a regular family in there, either farmers or maybe some successful big city people just wanting a nice country home.

But he had them, there. Their repeated attempts to have him declared insane had backfired, and he knew perfectly well his will would hold up in court. He'd willed the property to a total stranger, someone who'd commented online how much he admired the artwork, an 18-year-old kid from Sweden with a love of offensive art and bizarre, atonal music. The dragon would live.

So he sat, in the middle of a hot afternoon, at a table in his yard, observing the tangle all around, and listening to the hum of the insects and the occasional clank of wind chimes, sipping at a tall, chilled glass of water, and hitting on a big, fat joint, which he had a barrel full of. "Yeah," he said to himself out loud. "Life is good."

Acknowledgements

*I have always talked and thought about this book as
a Utopian novel. In it, I present solutions to hunger,
homelessness, war, injustice, oppression, traffic jams, road
rage, parking, desertification, soil degradation, littering,
illiteracy, lack of health care, refugees, floods, drought,
wildfires, hurricanes, and the threat of a rogue asteroid
striking the Earth.*

*Maybe, though, it's more of a manifesto than a novel. I
mean, it has characters, a story of sorts, a beginning,
middle and ending, and it's a nice,*

*neat length for a short novel, but there's not a lot of tension
or deep dive character development, and there are no car
chases, tavern brawls, parking lot shootouts or pretty
teenaged girls chained up in basements. You just wouldn't
have those things in a Utopian society. Which might
explain why there is so much more dystopian than utopian
fiction out there.*

*Whatever it is, here it is, and I would like to thank
all the people who volunteered to proofread it for me,
particularly Lance Von Beelitz, Daniel Lamken, and my
brother Dennis Watson, who all read it and left several*

constructive comments.

Also my wife, Helena, for her invaluable help in putting the book together for publication. I couldn't have done it without you, Sugar Plum.

Our daughter, Isabel, gets credit for the cover design.

9 79 8 3 3 8 0 2 8 7 9 7